Issues and Debates in Cyberpsychology

Issues and Debates in Cyberpsychology

Linda K. Kaye

Open University Press

Open University Press
McGraw Hill
8th Floor, 338 Euston Road
London
England
NW1 3BH

email: enquiries@openup.co.uk
world wide web: www.openup.co.uk

and Two Penn Plaza, New York, NY 10121-2289, USA

First published in this edition 2022

A catalogue record of this book is available from the British Library

ISBN-13: 9780335250776
ISBN-10: 0335250777
eISBN: 9780335250783

Library of Congress Cataloging-in-Publication Data
CIP data applied for

Typeset by Transforma Pvt. Ltd., Chennai, India

PRAISE

Technology is neither positive or negative, and indeed our lives are not simply online or offline. This book sheds light on the intricate interweaving of technology through every aspect of our lives and the impact this has on society.

With its accessible presentation style and its focus on "scientifically sound" practices, this book benefits the public, students, and researchers alike. It helps to understand the evidence underpinning contemporary issues related to technology use through an exploration of the inconsistencies, weaknesses, gaps and opportunities in the research to date. It seeks to motivate researchers to move beyond simply measuring time spent using technology as an indicator of behaviour, to authentically ask what people are doing with and through technology, why, how and to what end. Understanding the relationship between user needs, motivations, experiences and how these are best fulfilled through technology, will ameliorate unintended negative consequences in the future.

Prof Lynne Coventry, Director of PactLab,
University of Northumbria, UK

This is an engaging book with an accessible writing style. Relevant issues are explored by examining the evidence for key debates in the area, rather than the more usual topic based style, which works really well. The 'what-how-why' framework (WHW) presents a useful way to develop understanding, and the regular thinking activities and take home messages provide an opportunity to engage with the content more deeply and to summarise what has been covered so far. This book is a valuable guide to anyone seeking to further explore current thinking in the field.

Dr Rachel Harrad, Lecturer in Psychology,
Swansea University, UK

This book provides an accessible and engaging introduction to a wide range of key contemporary issues in cyberpsychology. It summarises psychological theories and empirical literature in a balanced, objective way – cutting through some of the myths and assumptions about the topics that prevail in the media and public perceptions. It does not tell the reader what to think, but walks them through the existing evidence base, encouraging them to take a critical perspective and make up their own minds.

Dr Joanne Lloyd, Senior Lecturer in Cyberpsychology,
University of Wolverhampton UK

This book consolidates a range of perspectives and debates that have been floating around the area of Cyberpsychology for some time and summarises these complex issues in a balanced, evidenced, and accessible way. The book is relevant and timely and is a call to action that inspires working towards a common direction to address and engage with these issues going forward, which will be of interest to researchers and practitioners new to the field as well as those who have been working in this area for a long time.

Dr. Maša Popovac, Lecturer in Psychology,
University of Buckingham, UK

The evolution of the internet and technology has created some of the most complex and important challenges for humanity. Research on any particular issue seldom provides clear guidance with contradictory findings or out-dated implications. In this book, Kaye tackles this challenge by bringing together, and critically reviewing a broad range of issues and debates. Each chapter examines the evidence behind major claims and concerns in specific domains. Importantly, the chapters are structured together in a way that allows for the emergence of themes that guide a broader psychological understanding of how humans interact with technology.

Brendan Rooney, Director of the Media and
Entertainment Psychology Lab, School of Psychology,
University College Dublin, Ireland

Contents

Acknowledgements

I'm not quite sure whether agreeing to write my first book during the period of a global pandemic was a stroke of genius or idiocy. Either way, here it is in all its glory. Overall, this has been a really rewarding experience. Certainly, I have found it useful to draw together and articulate a lot of what otherwise buzzes around my head. Additionally, the process of writing these thoughts down has helped crystallise my thinking on these issues, which can only be beneficial for my ongoing adventures in cyberpsychology.

There are so many people who should be celebrated here as a part of these acknowledgements. I don't have space to name you all – but no matter, you all know who you are. I do, however, wish to specifically thank my mum, dad, and twin sister: Joan, Jon, and Joanne (they obviously ran out of Js when they got to me) for everything.

I make it my mission in life to enthuse, engage, and inspire. If I can achieve any one of these in my life's activities with others, I know I'm doing something right. I hope that this book will indeed enthuse, engage, and/or inspire you.

1 Introduction

Welcome to the exciting world of cyberpsychology! This book will provide insights into the range of key issues and debates in cyberpsychology to help you navigate the current evidence-base to draw some informed conclusions about the role of technology for individuals and society. The book is structured under four thematic headings: 'Concepts', 'Uses', 'Effects', and 'Society', each of which includes a series of chapters designed to introduce key debates in the field. I chose this particular format as there is no other cyberpsychology text that consolidates the literature through the perspective of key cyberpsychology debates. Most current books are structured more thematically by topic area to outline the key theories and insights. Whilst these have played a critical role in progressing the field, I felt that a book which situates the evidence around key debates could provide a useful 'go-to' guide for those seeking to resolve ongoing societal and academic debates. Whilst the book does not address all the current issues and debates or indeed all cyberpsychology topics, I have selected those that remain most relevant to contemporary Western debate and societal interest. As is the case with the wider discipline of psychology and other cyberpsychology resources, the book will largely adopt a Western perspective on the issues.

Within the field of cyberpsychology, there are ongoing conceptual and practical issues, so one of the objectives of this book is to identify these within relevant chapters and note practical recommendations as appropriate. In the general absence of solid conceptual frameworks, we may be compromising methodological validity in our measurement of cyberpsychological phenomena. Whilst core psychological frameworks can be drawn upon to establish how these apply in the cyberpsychology domain, it is also the case that these will not always be relevant or appropriate to all the issues we study. Cyberpsychology can continue to progress with ongoing conceptual care and scrutiny. In the spirit of this, Chapter 2 forms Part 1, 'Concepts', in which I introduce cyberpsychology as a field, distinguish it from other cognate disciplines, outline some of the prominent perspectives in the field, and provide an account of how I see the role of debate in advancing scientific and societal understanding of the issues. This sets up subsequent chapters, which handle specific conceptual issues in more detail and move the discussion to how these are perhaps best resolved.

Part 2, 'Uses', begins with a chapter on 'technology use'. In it, I start by outlining the various conceptualisations of what we may mean by technology 'use'. Within the literature, this has been conceptualised in different ways within different fields and so I present a conceptual framework that outlines how these disparate perspectives could be better integrated. This includes the literature on technology uses and gratification, technology acceptance, affordances, behaviours, engagement, as well as overuse. Better conceptual integration here can afford us a much better understanding of what we mean when we refer to 'technology use' and its various components and processes.

Chapter 4 addresses 'online citizenship' and is intended to help answer some societal questions, such as 'why is our behaviour different online than in the real world?' I start by outlining the discourses around the way we describe our online experiences. In particular, I highlight the potential issues we face when we consider our online behaviours as being entirely separate from the self or our 'real-world' contexts. The chapter then moves on to find resolution in a number of debates which underpin this, such as the dubious 'digital native' vs. 'digital immigrant' debate. This is followed by a critical consideration of how debates which seek to compare categories of behaviour as 'online' vs. 'offline' are limited in addressing meaningful phenomena.

Chapter 5, the last of the three chapters in Part 2, addresses the issue of 'screen-time vs. screen use'. Whilst on the surface these may appear to refer to the same thing, I discuss the ways in which the two can be conceptualised and therefore measured in distinct ways. I begin with a brief outline of the conceptual challenges in 'screen-time' debates, and move on to distinguish how 'uses' may be the underpinning functions which 'screen-time' can seek to measure. I provide a conceptual framework with indicative behaviours to illustrate where these distinctions may be realised, with suggestions around measurement.

Having so far been concerned with a range of relevant issues and debates as to how we understand different types of use and behaviour in relation to technology and the internet, Part 3, 'Effects', is where we really start to drill down to some of the pertinent societal debates. As concerns about the effects of technology and the internet are widespread in society, Chapters 6–9 tackle some of the relevant issues. Chapter 6 advances the issues noted in Chapter 5, by discussing the existing evidence about the so-called effects of 'screen-time'. This goes some way to address current questions, such as 'how does screen-time relate to mental health?' The chapter presents existing knowledge of the effects of technology and the internet on physical health and psychosocial functioning, and provides a critical perspective of the way in which researchers might best advance their efforts in this area. In general, I recommend retiring a 'screen-time' approach and instead concerning ourselves with specific uses and behaviours that are more psychologically interesting and insightful.

Chapters 7 and 8 focus more specifically on social media to discuss 'social media and relationships' (Chapter 7) and 'social media and well-being' (Chapter 8). Chapter 7 poses the question, 'how "real" are online friends?', and goes on to illuminate debates about how social media (and online relationships more generally) are often considered the 'poor relation' of human relationships. After introducing theoretical perspectives to help understand these issues, I then pose the rather obvious question, 'how social is social media?', which, it seems, lacks a substantial evidence-base at the time of writing. To draw out some practical considerations, I review the evidence to help underpin the range of ways we can be 'social' on social media. This is intended to advance scholarship in the field, where the focus can be more on the behaviours and interactions on social media rather than 'social media use' *per se*.

Following on from a focus on relationships, Chapter 8 addresses 'social media and well-being'. This is important given the deep societal interest in this issue to help answer questions such as, 'is social media making us depressed?'. Here, I present a conceptual framework that advances our understanding of these issues. It applies the 'what', the 'how' (outlined in Chapter 7), and the 'why' (WHW framework) of social media use, to illustrate how these are prerequisites to add nuance to understanding how these relate to aspects of well-being.

Chapter 9, the final chapter of Part 3, is on 'digital games effects'. Similar to Chapter 8, the effects of digital games are well represented in everyday societal debate. Chapter 9 begins by posing the question, 'do violent video games make us aggressive?'. The chapter takes a similar approach to Chapter 8, and breaks down the debates around the effects of digital games by considering the 'what', the 'how', the 'why', as well as the 'where' and the 'who' of this phenomenon. This provides a useful conceptual approach to better account for how digital games may relate to said effects.

In Part 4, 'Society', I address the public and societal-facing role of cyberpsychology. In Chapter 10, titled 'Using online data', I look at what is meant by online data, given that this can refer to many things. I outline the ethical implications of how consent operates in the way we provide online data. The remainder of the chapter outlines the range of ways online data is used in varying contexts such as legal uses, security uses, and commercial uses. This illuminates the extensive range of online data which exists and how cyberpsychology may intercept some of these to better understand contemporary human behaviour.

The final substantive chapter is Chapter 11, titled 'Cyberpsychology in the world'. It highlights the role of cyberpsychology outside academic spheres. Here I make reference to its role in media and public debate, policy and practice. For each of these, I use examples largely from my own experience to illuminate how cyberpsychology insights can directly impact on these processes. In an ever-evolving technological world, the role of cyberpsychology will grow and therefore I argue for making it more visible in society.

To draw things to a close, the concluding chapter provides some reflections on the future of cyberpsychology. Here, I identify what advancements in theoretical and practical elements are required. To initiate the latter of these, I provide a pragmatic framework with example research questions to help start such a movement. Whilst this is by no means intended to be exhaustive or sufficient, I believe it may be of help to researchers in their subsequent research planning.

PART 1

Concepts

2 What is cyberpsychology?

The British Psychological Society (BPS) describes cyberpsychology as 'a scientific inter-disciplinary domain that focuses on the psychological phenomena which emerge as a result of the human interaction with digital technology, particularly the internet' (BPS, 2019). Cyberpsychology is a sub-discipline of psychology, within which we apply core theoretical principles to online settings and, in some cases, seek to derive new theoretical understanding of these experiences. In this sense, it is both an application of the psychology that we know, as well as a pioneering area that is developing new knowledge of human behaviour. When defining technology and the internet, this can cover a broad range of examples. Technology largely refers to devices such as smartphones, tablets, PCs, games, and gaming consoles. The internet is the infrastructure of connectivity that draws these technologies together (Attrill-Smith, Fullwood, Keep, & Kuss, 2019). This is distinct from the 'World Wide Web', which is instead the tool through which we access domains available on the internet (Attrill-Smith et al., 2019).

A number of interchangeable terms are evident in work in this area. The terms 'digital', 'online', 'net', 'tele', 'virtual', 'e-', and 'cyber' are often used to refer to the same notion but perhaps require further scrutiny. Arguably, 'digital' and 'e-' (short for 'electronic') do not necessitate internet connectivity in the same way as the others do. 'Digital' is often used when referring to things like 'digital literacy' and 'digital divide', which typically relate to knowledge pertaining to technology and its affordances. 'e-' is often used when referring to everyday activities which may have an electronic alternative, such as e-health, e-commerce, and e-fitness. Interestingly, these usually do require internet connectivity to fulfil tasks, yet the 'e' is now considered a somewhat 'old-fashioned' prefix. The term 'net' has largely become extinct in the literature, although sometimes it is used to describe the 'net generation'. 'Online', 'cyber', and 'virtual' are most often used interchangeably and can be considered to refer to the same thing. Interestingly, for some concepts, one term tends to be favoured over others, such as 'cyber-sex', as we rarely see reference to 'virtual sex' or 'online sex'. However, in other cases different prefixes may be used to refer to the same concept (e.g. cyber-bullying and online bullying). For the purposes of this book, I will use online, cyber, and virtual interchangeably and restrict my use of other terms in an attempt to avoid confusion.

There is some confusion about how cyberpsychology is different from human-computer interaction (HCI), which is a well-established field and which also arguably draws together the interactions between humans and technology. HCI tends to focus more on the interaction between the human and the machine, by exploring the interactivity and usability of systems such as computers. It has a key focus on the design, implementation, and evaluation of the computing systems that humans use. This, in my view, is how cyberpsychology differs from HCI. Cyberpsychology has more traditionally been focused on the effects and impacts of technology use and the internet, and not contributed so much to our understandings of the components of use itself. This is illustrated by the fact that HCI overlaps strongly with areas such as user experience (UX) design and user-centred design (UCD), which are strongly centred on the capacity and efficacy of systems, whereas cyberpsychology often positions itself further away from these concerns. This is not to say that cyberpsychology is not relevant to these issues; on the contrary, it is entirely relevant, but has typically forged a path in parallel to these disciplines.

Other cognate sub-disciplines include cybernetics, which is perhaps more similar to HCI in its focus on the control and communication in the animal and machine (Wiener, 1948). In contrast, areas such as Media Psychology, Internet Psychology, and Web Psychology are seen to be more closely linked with cyberpsychology. Broadly speaking, cyberpsychology typically covers three main areas: (1) our motivations for using technology and aspects of the internet; (2) how we interact with others using technology and the internet; and (3) the effects and impacts associated with using technology and the internet. This is distinct from fields such as Media Psychology, for example, which is more concerned with the impacts of media consumption on an individual and societal level.

Taking these three main areas of cyberpsychology, we can start to map out common trends and paradigms that are prevalent within the field. First, the study of motivations for using technology and aspects of the internet largely seeks to understand why people choose to use or engage in certain online activities or behaviours. Popular conceptual approaches to this area include uses and gratifications theory (LaRose & Eastin, 2004; LaRose, Mastro, & Eastin, 2001) and mood management theory (Zillmann, 1988a, 1988b; Zillmann & Bryant, 1985), although these are probably more central to media psychology. Interestingly, these tend to relate to using or engaging in certain online behaviours or activities but not so much to using technological devices themselves. In line with this, there is a substantial literature focused on technology adoption utilising theories such as the 'Technology Acceptance Model' (Marangunić & Granić, 2015), which is a socio-cognitive theory of the factors that encourage people to initiate technology use. However, this does not tend to readily enter into the scope of cyberpsychology and instead sits more centrally in technology and education. I discuss technology use and these perspectives in further detail in Chapter 3. Interestingly, a lot of the literature on our motivations for using technology and the internet tends to situate this as an individually driven behaviour. However, this tends to overlook the fact that technology use largely operates at the societal, political, and economic levels, limiting how these theories can be used to fully understand technology use in the twenty-first century.

The second main area in cyberpsychology relates to human interactions online, where we explore issues such as how our online interactions vary from our 'real-world' interactions, and how this relates to the quality of our relationships and social ties. Many of the debates surrounding this are situated in the sub-area of computer-mediated communication (CMC). CMC largely refers to human communication that occurs between two or more electronic devices, via email, instant messaging, chat rooms, text messaging, or social networking sites. CMC became very popular upon the development of Web 2.0, which was a much more functional and interactive environment for users and thus was better equipped to host interaction between users. Most research in this area has focused on asynchronous vs. synchronous interaction, online vs. offline communication, paralinguistic aspects of CMC (e.g. emoji, textisms), and how CMC potentially alters human behaviour relative to 'real-world' settings. I cover some of this in Chapter 4. Popular theoretical perspectives in this area include hyper-personal theory (Walther, 1996), displacement hypothesis vs. stimulation hypothesis (Neuman, 1988; Valkenburg & Peter, 2009), social capital theory (Putnam, 2000), and the online disinhibition effect. The majority of these will be covered further in Chapter 7. However, much of the aforementioned issues about online interactions are focused on human-human interactions and less so on interactivity in intelligent systems or with algorithms. These issues are pertinent to twenty-first century interactions and communication.

The third main area of cyberpsychology, arguably the principal area of societal debate, is that of the impacts of technology and internet use. Here, research looks at the association between the amount and type of use, with psychosocial variables relating to both positive and negative well-being. Recent theoretical perspectives which lend themselves to this debate include the Digital Goldilocks hypothesis (Przybylski & Weinstein, 2017), which I look at in Chapter 8. The debates here remain highly volatile and pertinent in a society that is concerned about the harmful effects of technology, and the role of cyberpsychology here is very important. More is discussed on the role of cyberpsychology for public debate in Chapter 11. A general observation here is that a lot of the discussion is devoted to the volume of technology use (time spent using, frequency of use) but arguably this is not especially enlightening when theorising about potential psychological and social effects.

Another major limitation of the 'technology effects' literature, particularly when theorising about behavioural outcomes, is a general lack of focus on theoretical models underpinning behaviour change. That is, behaviour is vastly complex and motivated by a broad range of factors, as is acknowledged in most theoretical models of behaviour change, including the 'COM-B system' (Michie, van Stralen, & West, 2011) and the Theory of Planned Behaviour (Ajzen, 1985, 1991; Ajzen & Madden, 1986). As such, technology effects perspectives that theorise that technologies lead to behavioural outcomes or changes would benefit from further integration of these scientific insights.

Whilst the above areas are not an exhaustive list, they do broadly cover the key approaches and issues addressed by cyberpsychology. A theme common to all these is the methodological approach taken by researchers. Self-report cross-sectional survey methodology dominates cyberpsychology (Howard & Jayne, 2015), meaning research may be limited by inaccurate estimates of technology usage behaviour (Ellis, 2019; Sewall, Bear, Merranko, & Rosen, 2020), poorly developed psychometric scales (Howard & Jayne, 2015), and limited knowledge of long-term effects (Kaye, Orben, Ellis, Hunter, & Houghton, 2020). There are vast opportunities to advance cyberpsychology insights by applying greater rigour and attention to its conceptual foundations and methodological approaches. Further discussion of these issues will be found in Chapters 3, 5, and 6.

One of my key motivations for writing this book is the tendency to assume the existence of dichotomies in this area of study, with any debate regrettably becoming polarised. Whilst I am not against debate in principle (indeed, this can be a key part of advancing perspectives and understanding of issues), what I struggle with is the tendency for society (and researchers) to create dichotomies in the rhetoric surrounding technology and internet use, largely in relation to their impact. In terms of research, it is evident that the epistemological perspectives we adopt drive our conceptual assumptions about technology use and its impacts. This is not unique to cyberpsychology, but evident across disciplines and sectors. In the case of technology use and impacts, we often see a divide between the 'technology for good' perspective and 'technology is harmful' perspective. Dunbar (2016) uses the terms 'cyberpessimists' and 'cyberoptimists' to distinguish between the adherents of these two perspectives when discussing the effect of the internet on our social lives, for example. Unfortunately, adding to the mix is the tendency for society to lean towards a technology panics rhetoric, which has been evident throughout the technological revolution. In this 'Sisyphean cycle of technology panics' (Orben, 2020), any new technology tends to create societal panic, motivating researchers to attempt to study it, but scientific progress is too slow to help inform policy and public understanding and so the panic persists. Whilst individual researchers may have their own epistemological take on these issues and opt to take a certain 'side' in the debate, it may come as a shock to some that these perspectives can actually exist side by side when teasing out the nuances of the issue. For example, in the case of social media effects (which we will be covered in further detail in Chapter 8), benefits and harms are both conceivable yet dependent on a number of factors, such as:

- **What?** – what content people are being exposed to. If two people are using the same social media platform for the same amount of time, but seeing different content, this may lead to two entirely different outcomes. In some cases, some of this content could be harmful and this, of course, is an area for concern.
- **How?** – how much people are using. Irrespective of content, the amount people are using and the level of their interactions with others will likely have an impact on any well-being outcomes.
- **Why?** – irrespective of what the content or actual usage is, people use social media for different reasons. For some people this may be the only way of fulfilling social needs, whereas for others it may be a helpful supplement.

I thus propose the WHW framework ('what-how-why' framework), and whilst this isn't exactly revolutionary as a name, it serves the purpose of supporting efforts in this area. This reflects other recent commentary about these issues in which a distinction has been made between technology-centred and user-centred approaches (Meier & Reinecke, 2020). Namely, technology-centred approaches tend to focus almost exclusively on volume of use (time, frequency), whereas user-centred approaches focus more on why people use technology. Interestingly, a lot of existing cyberpsychology research focuses on measuring the former as a way of exploring how technology use relates to psychological outcomes, yet the user-centred questions actually seem more psychologically interesting.

Adopting a more user-centred perspective may be one way of reducing the apparent dichotomy to help progress our understanding of the phenomena at hand. Certainly, epistemological positions which largely relate to technology-centred approaches tend to lead researchers to select certain theoretical perspectives over others. For example, those who view technology as bad may fail to recognise the affordances it can provide. They may therefore elect to explore technology from the displacement perspective, demonstrating how spending time using technology and the internet is reducing the time spent on more 'meaningful' activities. Results in line with this therefore will illuminate the negative role of technology on individuals and society. However, those seeking to evidence the benefits of technology may instead seek to further understand the specific technological uses, affordances, and behaviours which enrich our lives and thus may have a positive impact. The purpose of this book is to provide a review and resolution based on our current knowledge and evidence of these issues, to draw out the key learning points in moving forward in a more coordinated fashion. Certainly debates will continue to prevail in cyberpsychology, but reducing polarisation and dichotomies in thinking can be a helpful way of moving the field forward. This advancement is not only scientifically and academically important, but also pertinent to support societal debate and public policy. Indeed, Chapter 11 will elucidate the specifics of this issue and draw attention to why a critical synthesis of available evidence is paramount to informing public debate and discourse. Cyberpsychology is therefore critical in addressing the current confusion and contradictions in existing academic and public debates.

References

Ajzen, I. (1985). From intentions to actions: A theory of planned behavior. In J. Kuhl & J. Beckmann (Eds.), *Action control* (pp. 11–39). Berlin: Springer.

Ajzen, I. (1991). The theory of planned behavior. *Organizational Behavior and Human Decision Processes, 50* (2), 179–211. https://doi.org/10.1016/0749-5978(91)90020-T

Ajzen, I., & Madden, T.J. (1986). Prediction of goal-directed behavior: Attitudes, intentions, and perceived behavioral control. *Journal of Experimental Social Psychology, 22* (5), 453–474. https://doi.org/10.1016/0022-1031(86)90045-4

Attrill-Smith, A., Fullwood, C., Keep, M., & Kuss, D. (2019). *Oxford handbook of cyberpsychology.* Oxford: Oxford University Press.

British Psychological Society (BPS) (2019). *Cyberpsychology Section.* Retrieved 17 July 2020 from: https://www.bps.org.uk/member-microsites/cyberpsychology-section

Dunbar, R. (2016). Do online social media cut through the constraints that limit the size of offline social networks? *Royal Society Open Science, 3,* 150292. https://doi.org/10.1098/rsos.150292

Ellis, D.A. (2019). Are smartphones really that bad? Improving the psychological measurement of technology-related behaviors. *Computers in Human Behavior, 97,* 60–66. https://doi.org/10.1016/j.chb.2019.03.006

Howard, M.C., & Jayne, B.S. (2015). An analysis of more than 1,400 articles, 900 scales, and 17 years of research: The state of scales in cyberpsychology, behavior, and social networking. *Cyberpsychology, Behavior and Social Networking, 18* (3), 181–187. https://doi.org/10.1089/cyber.2014.0418

Kaye, L.K., Orben, A., Ellis, D.A., Hunter, S.C., & Houghton, S. (2020). The conceptual and methodological mayhem of 'screen-time'. *International Journal of Environmental Research and Public Health, 17* (10), 3661. https://doi.org/10.3390/ijerph17103661

LaRose, R., & Eastin, M.S. (2004). A social cognitive theory of Internet uses and gratifications: Toward a new model of media attendance. *Journal of Broadcasting and Electronic Media, 48* (3), 358–377. https://doi.org/10.1207/s15506878jobem4803_2

LaRose, R., Mastro, D., & Eastin, M.S. (2001). Understanding Internet usage: A social-cognitive approach to uses and gratifications. *Social Science Computer Review, 19* (4), 395–413. https://doi.org/10.1177/089443930101900401

Marangunić, N., & Granić, A. (2015). Technology acceptance model: A literature review from 1986 to 2013. *Universal Access in the Information Society, 14* (1), 81–95. https://doi.org/10.1007/s10209-014-0348-1

Meier, A., & Reinecke, L. (2020). Computer-mediated communication, social media and mental health: A conceptual and empirical meta-review. *Communication Research.* https://doi.org/10.1177/0093650220958224

Michie, S., van Stralen, M.M., & West, R. (2011). The behaviour change wheel: A new method for characterising and designing behaviour change interventions. *Implementation Science, 6,* 42. https://doi.org/10.1186/1748-5908-6-42

Neuman, S.B. (1988). The displacement effect: Assessing the relation between television viewing and reading performance. *Reading Research Quarterly, 23* (4), 414–440. https://doi.org/10.2307/747641

Orben, A. (2020). The Sisyphean cycle of technology panics. *Perspectives in Psychological Science, 15* (5), 1143–1157. https://doi.org/10.1177/1745691620919372

Przybylski, A.K., & Weinstein, N. (2017). A large-scale test of the Goldilocks hypothesis: Quantifying the relations between digital-screen use and the mental well-being of adolescents. *Psychological Science, 28* (2), 204–215. https://doi.org/10.1177/0956797616678438

Putnam, R.D. (2000). *Bowling alone.* New York: Simon & Schuster.

Sewall, C.J.R., Bear, T.M., Merranko, J., & Rosen, D. (2020). How psychosocial well-being and usage amount predict inaccuracies in retrospective estimates of digital technology use. *Mobile Media & Communication, 8* (3), 379–399. https://doi.org/10.1177/2050157920902830

Valkenburg, P.M., & Peter, J. (2009). Social consequences of the Internet for adolescents: A decade of research. *Current Directions in Psychological Science, 18,* 1–5. https://doi.org/10.1111/j.1467-8721.2009.01595.x

Walther, J.B. (1996). Computer-mediated communication: Impersonal, interpersonal, and hyperpersonal interaction. *Communication Research, 23* (1), 3–43. https://doi.org/10.1177/009365096023001001

Wiener, N. (1948). *Cybernetics: Or control and communication in the animal and the machine.* New York: The Technology Press/Wiley.

Zillmann, D. (1988a). Mood management: Using entertainment to full advantage. In L. Donohew, H.E. Sypher, & E.T. Higgins (Eds.), *Communication, social cognition and affect* (pp. 147–171). Hillsdale, NJ: Lawrence Erlbaum Associates.

Zillmann, D. (1988b). Mood management through communication choices. *American Behavioral Scientist, 31* (3), 327–340. https://doi.org/10.1177/000276488031003005

Zillmann, D., & Bryant, J. (1985). Affect, mood, and emotion as determinants of selective exposure. In D. Zillmann & J. Bryant (Eds.), *Selective exposure to communication* (pp. 157–190). Hillsdale, NJ: Lawrence Erlbaum Associates.

PART 2

Uses

3 | Technology use

'Technology use' is a very broad term and potentially can describe the way we use and engage with any type of technological or electronic device. The broadness of the term becomes problematic when teasing out the conceptual and operational facets of this phenomenon. For example, we can consider the term 'use' in a number of different ways. First, whether you categorically 'use' a certain device or platform at all (e.g. Are you a Facebook user?, Do you use/own a smartphone?). Second, it may refer to the actual behaviours which take place on technology (e.g. using 'chat' features, use the 'stories' on Instagram, number of times you check your smartphone per day). Third, it can refer more broadly to your usage or engagement patterns (e.g. how much time you spend on TikTok per day, whether or not you use Twitter for professional networking). Finally, 'use' is often conflated with attitudes towards a technology (e.g. On a scale of 1 to 5, how much do you enjoy using Twitter?). This presents a practical issue when attempting to consolidate the main findings in the literature. To provide a framework for the rest of the chapter, I have developed Figure 3.1 to better outline the various relevant aspects when discussing technology use.

When seeking to understand technology use, it is first useful to know why it is being used – this forms the first part of Figure 3.1, *affordances*.[1] In basic terms, this poses the question: 'How is using this technology going to help me fulfil a specific need?' As noted in Chapter 2, this is largely underpinned by the uses and gratifications perspective (LaRose & Eastin, 2004; LaRose, Mastro, & Eastin, 2001). For example, recent work has applied this perspective to

Figure 3.1. Model of factors relevant to understanding 'technology use'

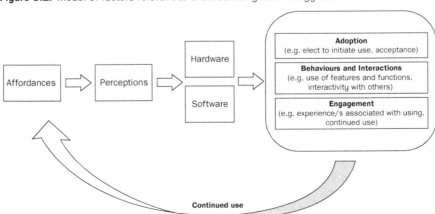

understand smartphone use (Hiniker, Patel, Kohno, & Kientz, 2016). Hiniker et al. make a distinction between 'instrumental' and 'ritualistic' purposes, whereby the former are goal-directed and purposeful whereas the latter are habitual. Other work using a uses and gratifications perspective has shown that these underlying motivations play a key role in determining the usage and behaviours associated with the technological activity (Hilvert-Bruce, Neill, Sjöblom, & Hamari, 2018). For example, the extent to which users' motivations for social media live-streaming are gratified by the platform, determines usage behaviour such as time spent engaging in live-streaming and so on.

Whilst some uses may apply across a broad range of platforms or devices, others may be more specific to certain types of online activity. Escapism, for example, could be considered to be a motivation for many different technology and internet uses, but may operate as a more functional coping strategy in respect of some types of use, such as binge-watching (Halfmann & Reinecke, 2021). Therefore, the uses and gratifications perspective can provide a basis for mapping the actual *behaviours and interactions* people engage with, which forms a key part of understanding 'technology use' as shown in Figure 3.1.

The second part of Figure 3.1 relates to *perceptions*. This draws on insights from the technology acceptance and adoption literature, largely underpinned by the 'Technology Acceptance Model' (TAM; Marangunić & Granić, 2015). This model has been developed and extended considerably over the last few decades. In summary, it is a socio-cognitive model which seeks to explain the individual-level and contextual-level factors that encourage adoption of technology (Davis, Bagozzi, & Warshaw, 1989; Venkatesh, Morris, Davis, & Davis, 2003). Some of these relate to perceptions of the technology, such as perceived ease of use and usefulness, as well as contextual variables, such as facilitating conditions and social factors. The overarching principle of this model is that favourable perceptions of these factors will encourage intentions surrounding technology use, which will feed into continued use (Davis et al., 1989). In satisfying this, in the first instance this may be best referred to as technology 'adoption' but repeated return to this technology arguably is perhaps best referred to as 'continued use'. The point at which 'adoption' becomes 'use' is not well defined in the literature, but arguably the point at which an individual has accepted that a certain technology serves a gratification and adopts this over time is perhaps a useful way to characterise it. Recent work has attempted to synthesise the TAM (Shaw, Ellis, & Ziegler, 2018), as it has been noted that many researchers have simply added their own variables, resulting in one meta-analysis showing 78 external variables being common to the model (Yousafzai, Foxall, & Pallister, 2007). This has resulted in it being difficult to make generalisations about the principles of the model (Shaw et al., 2018). Therefore, recent work has synthesised this model in the form of the 'Technology Integration Model' (TIM), which draws together many of the socio-cognitive factors known to be relevant to the TAM, but also includes facets such as individual differences and technology extension and subtraction (Shaw et al., 2018). This refers to the extent to which a given technology has the affordances in place to extend a person's capabilities. In this sense, the TIM helps integrate the first two parts of Figure 3.1 to acknowledge the factors behind the process through which adoption may extend to continued use.

Interestingly, technology adoption as described above does not tend to feature centrally within cyberpsychology literature or debate, and instead exists in parallel as a largely independent entity, more common in literatures relating to educational or consumer technology. This is intriguing given the fact that it is a key part of understanding technology use and draws on psychological explanations for these behaviours. This is one example where conceptual synthesis and integration would be a fruitful endeavour.

In the final part of Figure 3.1, we have *technology usage*, where I have listed three key components: 'adoption' (previously discussed), 'behaviours and interactions', and 'engagement'. This addresses the various aspects of what are typically signposts when discussing 'technology use' but may represent quite different things.

Technology behaviours and interactions

'Behaviours and interactions' are perhaps what we are most interested in exploring in cyberpsychology. That is, we may wish to know how much we use social networking sites (SNSs), how many hours per week we watch TV, or what sort of features we use on SNSs. This information is often used to understand the psychological correlates or impacts of technology use. This is where there is a high level of disparity in the academic literature. Usually it is the case that we get numerical metrics relating to volume of use. This may relate to *time* spent using in respect of a specific time reference point (hours/minutes used yesterday, last week), and *frequency* of use in a timed reference point (number of times smartphone was accessed per day). Regrettably, the literature is limited by a number of major issues. First, it is largely based on estimates and self-reported use; second, there is a mixture of time- and frequency-based metrics used to infer 'technology use'; and finally, there are a wide variety of time reference points used. These issues are discussed below.

When exploring technology use, particularly when volume is the metric of interest, it makes sense to obtain this information based on our actual use. After all, this information is readily available via screen-time apps and log data. However, cyberpsychology research has not fully capitalised on this, which is rather ironic given the subject area. Instead, the literature is heavily reliant on self-reports of use either in respect of users' average use or retrospectively with reference to a specific time-frame. Unfortunately, evidence suggests that this approach is problematic for the purposes of gaining accurate data on technology use (Andrews, Ellis, Shaw, & Piwek, 2015; Burnell, George, Kurup, Underwood, & Ackerman, 2021; Ellis, 2019; Ernala, Burke, Leavitt, & Ellison, 2020; Parry, Davidson, Sewall, Fisher, Mieczkowski, & Quintana, 2021; Sewall, Bear, Merranko, & Rosen, 2020; Verbeij, Pouwels, Beyens, & Valkenberg, 2021). A recent review illuminates that there are observable discrepancies between self-reported digital media use and the corresponding logged data (Parry et al., 2021). Additionally, it has been found that when comparing smartphone owners' estimates of their smartphone use and checking behaviours with objective data garnered from their smartphones, they grossly underestimate these behaviours (Andrews et al., 2015). Similarly for social networking sites, when comparing log data from Facebook with people's estimates of how much time they spend and number of log-ins per day, there are marked discrepancies (Ernala et al., 2020). That is, we tend to over-report how much time we spend on the platform, but under-report how many times we visit per day (Ernala et al., 2020). This is further corroborated by recent findings showing that across various platforms (Facebook, Instagram, Snapchat, and Twitter), we overestimate use (Burnell et al., 2021; Verbeij et al., 2021). To make things more complex, research has shown that there are various types of usage behaviours, such as 'checking' behaviour (e.g. smartphone used for less than 15 seconds), which are different from frequency of pick-ups or actual usage (Shaw, 2020). Inaccuracies also seem to arise depending on what technology or platform is being reported on. For example, iPhone users are less accurate at gauging their daily social media use than overall daily iPhone use (Sewall et al., 2020). In summary, making greater use of objective data garnered from technology itself would not only provide more accurate reports, but also put us in a stronger position to predict subsequent technology use (Ellis, Davidson, Shaw, & Geyer, 2019). Chapter 5 provides some suggestions of the types of specific behaviours which can be drawn from objective data of 'screen use' to help support these efforts.

As well as self-reported use being largely flawed as a measure of technology use, there appears to be little agreement as to how cyberpsychology researchers should measure technology use. Whilst some utilise time-framed reference points (e.g. minutes per day), others use frequency-based reference points (e.g. number of times per day). Furthermore, some garner 'total screen-time' in respect of a certain time-frame, while others ask participants to estimate the amount of screen-time on a typical day, and sometimes split this by weekday and weekend day, or school day and non-school day. The lack of standardisation on this somewhat basic issue is a cause for concern, especially when the findings from such research contributes so strongly to the current public debate on the impacts of technology. Recent evidence provides a rational basis for these concerns. For example, Ernala et al (2020) compared data from different types of self-reported Facebook use relative to server logs. These included time-based reports such as 'minutes per day', 'time per day', and 'daily time past week', as well as more general questions such as 'How much do you usually use Facebook?', which used various response options including endorsement scales (ranging from 'not at all' to 'a great deal') and relative to others (ranging from 'much less than most' to 'much more than most'). The authors found that, in general, people over-reported how much time they spent on Facebook and under-reported number of visits, thereby highlighting the wide variance and error in this approach to understanding technology use and behaviours.

Another prevalent concern in the technology use literature is the tendency of some research to use perception or attitude measures on Likert scales to obtain a measure of 'use'. This may consist either of asking supplementary measurements of usage by type of device or activity (e.g. passive use/TV viewing, social media use) or focusing more exclusively on one specific technology use or use of a specific platform or application. This may include questions about attitudes towards technology use that are then inferred as a proxy for screen-time, such as the Facebook Intensity Scale (Orosz, Tóth-Király, & Bőthe, 2016). Arguably, this is not a measure of 'use' (i.e. how much or how often) but rather experiences associated with use. Examples here include scale items such as 'mobile technology is a useful and effective tool in education' (Al-Emran, Elsherif, & Shaalan, 2016) and 'smartphones would be useful in medical education' (Robinson, Cronin, Ibrahim, Jinks, Molitor, Newman et al., 2013). Often, these are described as technology use, which adds additional levels of complexity to an already muddy conceptual field.

In summary, researchers who are exploring 'technology use' may be best using metrics garnered from objective log data or similar, to understand issues such as time or frequency of use, which may also be revealing of what specific types of interactions or behaviours occur. If attitudes or perceptions relating to technology use or engagement are the primary research question, then this may require the use of self-report attitude scales.

Technology engagement

To add further conceptual confusion to this field, the term 'technology engagement' is also used in the literature. Interestingly, this again does not feature prominently in the cyberpsychology literature but instead within educational technology and user-engagement literature. In respect of the former, 'technology engagement' is used to refer to conditions under which we show a willingness or tendency towards technology, such as 'students' engagement in technology-mediated learning' (e.g., Henrie, Halverson, & Graham, 2015). For example, in a paper titled 'Entangled with technology: Engagement with Facebook among the young old', Van House (2015) discusses 'engagement' in terms of whether people use or do not these technologies.

Alternatively, in relation to the user-engagement literature, of relevance to e-commerce and marketing, for example, 'engagement' appears to be used to refer to metrics demonstrating levels of success in consumers' uptake and continued use of technology. For example, work has conceptualised what engagement refers to and found that this consists of four stages: point of engagement, period of sustained engagement, disengagement, and re-engagement (O'Brien & Toms, 2008). In addition, engagement is also used to refer to the psychological experiences garnered through using technology (O'Brien & Toms, 2008). This is distinctly different from the notion of 'use' or some form of discrete measurable behaviour, and instead refers to the extent to which people are psychologically engaged or immersed during periods of use. For example, research has looked at engagement modes with information technology and how this relates to different profiles of users and flow experiences (Sharafi, Hedman, & Montgomery, 2006).

It would seem therefore that use and engagement, although arguably different constructs, are readily used interchangeably in the literature. A lack of conceptual clarity and consistency in the technology use literature makes it very difficult to navigate and understand the implications here for societal debate surrounding the impacts of technology use. In general, it appears that most of what we think we know about technology use and its effects, for example, is based on people's perceptions or their attitudes about using technology rather than their actual use. Arguably, these are quite different things.

Another key issue in this area is that there is a focus on volume as a metric, which perhaps is not especially interesting from a psychological perspective. Why are we so obsessed with time when studying the human experience with technology? It seems that there are far more interesting psychological questions we can be asking here.

When does use become overuse?

Despite technology use being a prevalent and functional part of twenty-first century living, a substantial proportion of the cyberpsychology literature is focused on pathological use of technology (e.g. Elhai, Dvorak, Levine, & Hall, 2017; Leung & Chen, 2018). Indeed, this is disproportionate to the estimated percentage of the population who are likely or at risk of being 'pathological users'. This has been driven by a group of dedicated researchers within the behavioural addiction field seeking to gain recognition of the potentially harmful and 'addictive' nature of technologies. To date, the only technology which has official clinical recognition (albeit alongside much debate about the validity of this) is that of 'gaming disorder', which was recently added to the ICD-11 (WHO, 2018). Beyond that, terms such as 'smartphone addiction' and 'social media addiction', which regularly appear both in the academic literature as well as the media, are not yet valid or clinically diagnosable labels to associate with technological experiences.

Exploring the cyberpsychology literature relating to pathological use highlights a number of issues. The first of these relates to interchangeable terminology. Taking 'internet addiction' as an example, it is not uncommon for any or all of the following terms to be used (in some cases, within the same journal article): 'problematic internet use', 'pathological internet use', 'excessive internet use', 'internet addiction disorder', internet use disorder', 'online addiction', and 'technological addiction' (Ryding & Kaye, 2018). Without a standardised term to refer to pathological use, this makes the literature difficult to navigate and our understanding of 'overuse' difficult to establish.

The second issue relates to the cut-off of what determines pathological (vs. 'normal') use. Studies in the area of pathological technology use typically apply polythetic classifications to determine this. For example, for an addiction scale with 10 items rated on a 5-point Likert scale (where 1= 'strongly disagree',

3 = 'neither disagree nor agree', and 5 = 'strongly agree'), a participant would have to respond 'neither disagree nor agree' (3) or higher on more than five items on the scale to be classed as an 'addict'. It is therefore entirely conceivable that a participant could respond that they 'neither disagree nor agree' with any of the statements on an addiction questionnaire but be classified as being addicted to the technology at hand. Recent research has highlighted the negative implications of this by developing a satirical 'offline friend addiction' scale, which replicates the approaches and scoring techniques for pathological technology use (Satchell, Fido, Harper, Shaw, Davidson, Ellis et al., 2021). The researchers revealed more than two-thirds of their sample could be considered to be addicted to their 'offline friends'. This corresponds to broader concerns in the field about the tendency for researchers to pathologise everyday behaviour (Billieux, Schimmenti, Khazaal, Maurage, & Heeren, 2015; Elhai, Yang, & Levine, 2020; Kardefelt-Winther, Heeren, Schimmenti, van Rooij, Maurage, Carras et al., 2017).

There are concerns about the extent to which technology 'addiction' scales are actually able to capture anything that is valid or of relevance to societal debate. When placing this in the context of the 'technology use' literature more generally, we can see that there is much disparity and conceptual confusion. That is, 'technology use' as a phenomenon is difficult to explore as a whole when there are such disparate conceptual and methodological perspectives used to explore it. These include socio-cognitive models of technological adoption that seek to understand perceptions of use, a wide range of flawed attempts to measure frequency and time spent using technology, and psychometric measures that potentially overstate what pathological use actually is. What is currently omitted is a more well-rounded integration of how these various sub-areas actually relate to one another, given that they are all attempting to measure the same phenomenon (albeit different aspects of this).

To understand pathological use or overuse, it is perhaps best approached from the perspective of how usage relates to needs and technological affordances (first part of Figure 3.1). We can draw on the insights of Hiniker et al. (2016) regarding instrumental vs. ritualistic/habitual use and how certain needs are gratified. For example, it could be the case that when technology use and behaviours address all of the relevant needs they are intended to serve, this could be considered healthy, 'normal' use. However, such balanced use would be upset in cases where technology use and behaviours exceed need gratification, and thus might be considered unhealthy or pathological use. Figure 3.2 illustrates this and may be underpinned by understanding how self-control or regulation of need fulfilment through technology use is maintained. Recent theoretical models allude to the issue of self-control, such as the Appraisal of Media Use, Self-Control, and Entertainment (AMUSE) model (Reinecke & Meier, 2021). This may go some way to represent the phenomenon more typically described as technology 'addiction', although caution is warranted here given that for this to be classed as 'addiction', usage should lead to specific detrimental impacts on psychological and social functioning.

Regrettably, little of the 'technology addiction' field integrates conceptual understanding of the more generic technology use literature to seek

Figure 3.2. Balancing technology use with needs/affordances

explanations of how these different balances of uses appear on a continuum. For example, how adoption leads to habitual use, which then may lead to pathological use. This requires a sharper focus on specific psychological and behavioural processes rather than a more generalised application of an addiction model (Billieux, Philippot, Schmid, Maurage, De Mol, & Van der Linden, 2014), thus offering a process-based approach to this issue. This is supported by recent papers highlighting that more is needed to understand the specific mechanisms behind why certain individuals may be 'at risk' of overuse (Elhai, Yang, & Montag, 2019; Elhai et al., 2020; Montag, Wegmann, Sariyska, Demetrovics, & Brand, 2020). This will help support the conceptual integration of technology adoption and use models with 'overuse' models, to draw together what are currently rather disparate fields.

Conclusion

This chapter has highlighted the complexities around the issue of 'technology use' and drawn out the various constituent aspects of this from a range of literatures, such as technology adoption/acceptance, uses and gratifications, social computation, and behavioural addiction. This has helped illuminate the challenges which cyberpsychology currently faces in understanding the phenomenon of 'technology use' from a unified perspective. I have argued that conceptual integration is an important step for us to take, and that there are many advancements needed when determining what 'technology use' actually refers to in operational terms.

Box 3.1: Thinking activity

Think about smartphones. Think back to your first smartphone.

- Why did you decide to purchase/inherit your first smartphone?
- What factors influenced you?
- Why have you continued to use it?
- If you were describing your current smartphone use, what would you say?

> **Box 3.2: Take-home message**
>
> Despite cyberpsychology researchers primarily being interested in technology interactions and effects, data from technology is typically not used in research! We therefore know little about the issue of technology use. Additionally, it is likely that what we think we know about the effects of smartphones and social media is not entirely accurate. We must remember that 'technology use' can refer to a lot of things and a complex process (adoption, continued use, specific usage behaviours, etc.) and finding conceptual agreement on how this fits together is paramount to move the field forward.

Note

1 'Affordances' and 'perceptions' can relate both to devices themselves (e.g. smartphones, tablets) and specific platforms or software (e.g. Facebook, educational software).

References

Al-Emran, M., Elsherif, H.M., & Shaalan, K. (2016). Investigating attitudes towards the use of mobile learning in higher education. *Computers in Human Behavior, 56*, 93–102. https://doi.org/10.1016/j.chb.2015.11.033

Andrews, S., Ellis, D.A., Shaw, H., & Piwek, L. (2015). Beyond self-report: Tools to compare estimated and real-world Smartphone use. *PLoS One, 10* (10), e0139004. https://doi.org/10.1371/journal.pone.0139004

Billieux, J., Philippot, P., Schmid, C., Maurage, P., De Mol, J., & Van der Linden, M. (2014). Is dysfunctional use of the mobile phone a behavioural addiction? Confronting symptom-based versus process-based approaches. *Clinical Psychology and Psychotherapy, 22* (5), 460–468. https://doi.org/10.1002/cpp.1910

Billieux, J., Schimmenti, A., Khazaal, Y., Maurage, P., & Heeren, A. (2015). Are we over-pathologizing everyday life? A tenable blueprint for behavioral addiction research. *Journal of Behavioral Addictions, 4*(3), 119–123. https://doi.org/10.1556/2006.4.2015.009

Burnell, K., George, M.J., Kurup, A.R., Underwood, M.K., & Ackerman, R.A. (2021). Associations between self-reports and device-reports of social networking site use: An application of the Truth and Bias model. *Communication Methods and Measures, 15* (2), 156–163. https://doi.org/10.1080/19312458.2021.1918654

Davis, F.D., Bagozzi, R.P., & Warshaw, P.R. (1989). User acceptance of computer technology: A comparison of two theoretical model authors. *Management Science, 35* (8), 982–1003. https://doi.org/10.1287/mnsc.35.8.982

Ellis, D.A. (2019). Are smartphones really that bad? Improving the psychological measurement of technology-related behaviors. *Computers in Human Behavior, 97*, 60–66. https://doi.org/10.1016/j.chb.2019.03.006

Ellis, D.A., Davidson, B.I., Shaw, H., & Geyer, K. (2019). Do smartphone usage scales predict behavior? *International Journal of Human-Computer Studies, 130*, 86–92. https://doi.org/10.1016/j.ijhcs.2019.05.004

Elhai, J.D., Dvorak, R.D., Levine, J.C., & Hall, B.J. (2017). Problematic smartphone use: A conceptual overview and systematic review of relations with anxiety and depression psychopathology. *Journal of Affective Disorders, 207*, 251–259. https://doi.org/10.1016/j.jad.2016.08.030

Elhai, J.D., Yang, H., & Levine, J.C. (2020). Applying fairness in labeling various types of internet use disorders: Commentary on How to overcome taxonomical problems in the study of internet use disorders and what to do with 'smartphone addiction'? *Journal of Behavioral Addictions, 9* (4), 924–927. https://doi.org/10.1556/2006.2020.00071

Elhai, J.D., Yang, H., & Montag, C. (2019). Cognitive- and emotion-related dysfunctional coping processes: Transdiagnostic mechanisms explaining depression and anxiety's relations with problematic smartphone use. *Current Addiction Reports, 6*, 410–417. https://doi.org/10.1007/s40429-019-00260-4

Ernala, S.K., Burke, M., Leavitt, A., & Ellison, N.B. (2020). How well do people report time spent on Facebook? An evaluation of established survey questions with recommendations. In *Proceedings of the 2020 CHI Conference on Human Factors in Computing Systems*, Honolulu, HI, 25–30 April. https://doi.org/10.1145/3313831.3376435

Halfmann, A., & Reinecke, L. (2021). Binge-watching as case of escapist entertainment use. In P. Vorderer & C. Klimmt (Eds.), *The Oxford handbook of entertainment theory* (pp. 181–203). Oxford: Oxford University Press.

Henrie, C.R., Halverson, L.R., & Graham, C.R. (2015). Measuring student engagement in technology-mediated learning: A review. *Computers and Education, 90* (1), 36–53. https://doi.org/10.1016/j.compedu.2015.09.005

Hilvert-Bruce, Z., Neill, J.T., Sjöblom, M., & Hamari, J. (2018). Social motivations of live-streaming viewer engagement on Twitch. *Computers in Human Behavior, 84*, 58–67. https://doi.org/10.1016/j.chb.2018.02.013

Hiniker, A., Patel, S.N., Kohno, T., & Kientz, J.A. (2016). Why would you do that? Predicting the uses and gratifications behind smartphone-usage behaviors. In P. Lukowicz & A. Kruger (Eds.), *UbiComp '16: Proceedings of the 2016 ACM International Joint Conference on Pervasive and Ubiquitous Computing* (pp. 634–645), Heidelberg, Germany. https://doi.org/10.1145/2971648.2971762

Kardefelt-Winther, D., Heeren, A., Schimmenti, A., van Rooij, A., Maurage, P., Carras, M., Edman, J., Blaszczynski, A., Khazaal, Y., & Billieux, J. (2017). How can we conceptualize behavioural addiction without pathologizing common behaviours? *Addiction, 112* (10), 1709–1715. https://doi.org/10.1111/add.13763

LaRose, R., & Eastin, M.S. (2004). A social cognitive theory of Internet uses and gratifications: Toward a new model of media attendance. *Journal of Broadcasting and Electronic Media, 48* (3), 358–377. https://doi.org/10.1207/s15506878jobem4803_2

LaRose, R., Mastro, D., & Eastin, M.S. (2001). Understanding Internet usage: A social-cognitive approach to uses and gratifications. *Social Science Computer Review, 19* (4), 395–413. https://doi.org/10.1177/089443930101900401

Leung, L., & Chen, C. (2018). A review of media addiction research from 1991 to 2016. *Social Science Computer Review.* https://doi.org/10.1177/0894439318791770

Marangunić, N., & Granić, A. (2015). Technology acceptance model: A literature review from 1986 to 2013. *Universal Access in the Information Society, 14* (1), 81–95. https://doi.org/10.1007/s10209-014-0348-1

Montag, C., Wegmann, E., Sariyska, R., Demetrovics, Z., & Brand, M. (2020). How to overcome taxonomical problems in the study of Internet use disorders and what to do with 'smartphone addiction'? *Journal of Behavioral Addictions, 9* (4), 908–914. https://doi.org/10.1556/2006.8.2019.59

O'Brien, H.L., & Toms, E.G. (2008). What is user engagement? A conceptual framework for defining user engagement with technology. *Journal of the American Society for*

Information Science and Technology, 59 (6), 938–955. https://doi.org/10.1002/asi.20801

Orosz, G., Tóth-Király, I., & Böthe, B. (2016). Four facets of Facebook intensity: The development of the Multidimensional Facebook Intensity Scale. *Personality and Individual Differences, 100*, 95–104. https://doi.org/10.1016/j.paid.2015.11.038

Parry, D., Davidson, B.I., Sewall, C., Fisher, J.T., Mieczkowski, H., & Quintana, D.S. (2021). A systematic review and meta-analysis of discrepancies between logged and self-reported digital media use. *Nature Human Behaviour.* https://doi.org/10.1038/s41562-021-01117-5

Reinecke, L., & Meier, A. (2021). Media entertainment as guilty pleasure? The Appraisal of Media Use, Self-Control, and Entertainment (AMUSE) model. In P. Vorderer & C. Klimmt (Eds.), *The Oxford handbook of entertainment theory* (pp. 205–230). Oxford: Oxford University Press.

Robinson, T., Cronin, T., Ibrahim, H., Jinks, M., Molitor, T., Newman, J., & Shapiro, J. (2013). Smartphone use and acceptability among clinical medical students: A questionnaire-based study. *Journal of Medical Systems, 37* (3), 9936. https://doi.org/10.1007/s10916-013-9936-5

Ryding, F.C., & Kaye, L.K. (2018). 'Internet addiction': A conceptual minefield. *International Journal of Mental Health and Addiction, 16* (1), 225–232. https://doi.org/10.1007/s11469-017-9811-6

Satchell, L., Fido, D., Harper, C., Shaw, H., Davidson, B.I., Ellis, D.A., Hart, C.M., Jalil, R., Jones, A., Kaye, L.K., Lancaster, G., & Pavetich, M. (2021). Development of an Offline-Friend Addiction Questionnaire (O-FAQ): Are most people really social addicts? *Behavior Research Methods, 53*, 1097–1106. https://doi.org/10.3758/s13428-020-01462-9

Sewall, C.J.R., Bear, T.M., Merranko, J., & Rosen, D. (2020). How psychosocial well-being and usage amount predict inaccuracies in retrospective estimates of digital technology use. *Mobile Media & Communication, 8* (3), 379–399. https://doi.org/10.1177/2050157920902830

Sharafi, P., Hedman, L., & Montgomery, H. (2006). Using information technology: Engagement modes, flow experience, and personality orientations. *Computers in Human Behavior, 22* (5), 899–916. https://doi.org/10.1016/j.chb.2004.03.022

Shaw, H. (2020). *Examining individual differences through 'everyday' smartphone behaviours: Exploring theories and methods.* Unpublished doctoral thesis. University of Lincoln, Lincoln.

Shaw, H., Ellis, D.A., & Ziegler, F.V. (2018). The Technology Integration Model (TIM): Predicting the continued use of technology. *Computers in Human Behavior, 83*, 204–214. https://doi.org/10.1016/j.chb.2018.02.001

Van House, N.A. (2015). Entangled with technology: Engagement with Facebook among the young old. *First Monday, 20* (11). https://doi.org/10.5210/fm.v20i11.6311

Venkatesh, V., Morris, M.G., Davis, G.B., & Davis, F.D. (2003). User acceptance of information technology: Toward a unified view. *MIS Quarterly, 27* (3), 425–478. https://doi.org/10.2307/30036540

Verbeij, T., Pouwels, J.L., Beyens, I., & Valkenberg, P.M. (2021). The accuracy and validity of self-reported social media use measures among adolescents. *Computers in Human Behavior Reports, 3*, 100090. https://doi.org/10.1016/j.chbr.2021.100090

World Health Organization (WHO) (2018). *Gaming disorder.* Retrieved 2 February 2018 from: https://icd.who.int/browse11/l-m/en#/http%3a%2f%2fid.who.int%2ficd%2fentity%2f1448597234

Yousafzai, S.Y., Foxall, G.R., & Pallister, J.G. (2007). Technology acceptance: A meta-analysis of the TAM: Part 1. *Journal of Modelling in Management, 2* (3), 251–280. https://doi.org/10.1108/17465660710834453

4 Online citizenship

Box 4.1: Current questions

- Why are people different online than in the real world?
- Does our behaviour change online?

There are a range of experiences we derive through living our lives online. In many ways, we can consider ourselves citizens of our virtual spaces, in which we occupy many different types of spaces in this arena. When we describe our citizenship with technology and online spaces, we tend to use a variety of terms which often vary based on the specific platform or type of space. For example, we mostly use the term 'users' to describe those who use technology. For example, 'I am an iPhone user' or 'I use Facebook'. However, this does not quite seem to capture the fact that we have life experiences which take place in these spaces, which is perhaps better represented by terms that refer to citizenship. An exception to this perhaps is that of Second Life, which is a 3D multi-user virtual world which uses the term 'residents' to refer to those who occupy this space. This seems more akin to the notion that life experiences are afforded to our virtual lives. The propositions we use to describe our engagements in different spaces or platforms are also interesting. We ask people, 'Are you *on* Facebook?' or 'I follow you *on* Twitter?', which does not quite situate ourselves as being fully immersed 'in' these spaces as citizens. Other terms we commonly see in virtual spaces relate to our networks and connections. Here we see a variety of terms used such as: 'friends' (Facebook), 'followers' (Instagram, Twitter, TikTok), 'members' (Facebook groups), and 'lists' (Twitter). The terminology here is interesting and suggests something about how we situate ourselves differently across different platforms and in correspondence to others.

Why are these issues important? I outline these as this helps us contextualise citizenship and how our experiences in virtual spaces are perhaps not quite seen as 'real' experiences in the way they would be in the 'real world'. This is important as the principles of this helps us understand why often in cyberpsychology, debates tend to focus on comparing online vs. offline behaviour. For example, people may seek to understand how our behaviour changes online, but tend to overlook the fact that the way we behave in many of our online settings is often simply an extension of our 'real-world' behaviours. In many cases, this implies that (1) our 'online' and 'offline' lives are mutually exclusive from one another, and (2) these are each homogeneous categories in themselves. Clearly, this is not the case on both counts. Let's look at each of these issues in more detail.

In respect of the first issue, it is simply not the case that our online and offline experiences are separate; rather, they are largely interrelated and entwined whereby the boundaries between them are becoming increasingly blurred and non-discrete. To illustrate the issues of describing 'online' and 'offline' as exclusive categories, we can look to a wide range of examples. A useful example is internet-enabled cybercrimes such as cyberstalking and cyberterrorism (Kirwan & Power, 2013), in which online behaviours have a clear interaction with and often consequences for our 'real-world' experiences or subsequent behaviours. Cybercrimes are just one example, but this principle extends to a wide range of everyday behaviours which intersect across contexts. An alternative and perhaps more useful approach to understanding citizenship involves considering how technology itself (and indeed our online representations) can be part of an extension or subtraction from the self (Shaw, Ellis, & Ziegler, 2018). For example, being part of a specific online gaming community allows us to extend that aspect of our identity by engaging in behaviours relevant in that context. It is the case we hold multiple social identities and these simply become more or less salient based on the context we currently occupy (Rydell & Boucher, 2010; Rydell, McConnell, & Beilock, 2009). In basic terms, we are not necessarily a different person online (a distinct 'online identity') but rather we engage in behaviours which allow us to express salient identities in those contexts irrespective of whether that is online or offline. Moving beyond thinking about 'selves' is the other important issue about how our behaviours do not remain exclusive to one or other context, but rather they interact. This is perhaps best illustrated by the notion of the 'Internet of Things', in which our internet-connected devices such as smartwatches and home security systems garner data of our *real-world* behaviour but in a way that is represented as *online* data. In this sense, it is impossible to detach the two.

In relation to the second issue, categorising 'online' as a homogeneous concept (e.g. online identity) fails to recognise that we operate as citizens in largely diverse ways across the range of online spaces we occupy. This further creates challenges for us when exploring virtual citizenship experiences and human behaviour. We rarely discuss our 'offline' behaviour as one category; we do not behave in the same way as spectators at a football match as we do when attending a church service. In the same vein, it is also meaningless to categorise our 'online behaviour' as homogeneous and unidimensional.

These underpinning issues form the basis for this chapter, which will address a number of key issues that are part of the cyberpsychology debate. The first is about unintended citizenship, whereby some individuals may find themselves represented online based on the behaviours of others. The second issue is that of 'digital natives' vs. 'digital immigrants', a rather unhelpful dichotomy that prevails unfortunately. I then move on to discuss issues around generational perspectives on technology use and the implications of its impacts. Again, I will challenge the value in this approach, especially in the context of informing public understanding and policy. Finally, I discuss issues surrounding the role of online settings in changing human inclinations and behaviour. This will be reviewed in light of my previous points about inferences being drawn by comparing simplistic categories of 'online' vs. 'offline' behaviour.

Unintended citizens

In twenty-first-century digital society, there are not many people who do not have a digital footprint of some sort. In most cases, we create these footprints through our engagements online, including via social media profiles and information. I discuss more about the online data we provide later in Chapter 10, particularly in relation to what constitutes online data based on our various behaviours. In brief, the terms 'active' and 'passive' digital footprint are typically used; the former refers to the traceable digital activities from an individual's deliberate actions, while the latter refers to the more subtle behaviours such as web-browsing, data left in cookies, and so on. However, an issue to note here is that there may be unintended citizens in the online world based on the information or behaviours others may share about them.

Let's take an example. It is Grandma's birthday and the family is celebrating the event. Grandma does not have a social networking profile but numerous family members have posted photos and information from the birthday event on their social networking site pages. All the people in those family members' networks and third-party social technology companies now have information about Grandma, potentially including personal information such as her date of birth. Therein, Grandma now has a digital footprint of sorts and is an unintended citizen in this space.

There are plenty of other examples, including infants and children who arguably are at the mercy of another party's perceptions of what constitutes consensual or appropriate information-sharing. Notwithstanding the ethical or moral implications of this, there are some interesting issues here with regard to who we define as a citizen in online spaces. Is it necessary for people themselves to have forged their own footprint to be considered as such, or is it sufficient that they have a footprint based on others' behaviours? In the context of digital footprints, this raises the question of whether an additional category is needed to extend the current ones of active and passive. Neither of these reflects the fact that others often contribute to our digital footprint. Whilst this is an 'active' form of footprint forging, it is not deliberate on the part of the individual themselves and therefore perhaps could be described as an 'indirect digital footprint'. Another way of creating an 'indirect' digital footprint is through services which rate people, such 'Rate my professor' or the controversial 'Peeple' app where people leave recommendations about others based on professional, personal, and romantic relationships. Why is this relevant? When we discuss online presence and citizenship, there are various levels on which we exist online. In some cases, this is via indirect digital footprints as described above, but also following death when our digital data and citizenship remain intact and we may largely operate as 'ghosts' in these spaces (Bassett, 2018; Kasket, 2020). Online citizenship is perhaps a little more complex than it may seem on the surface. The remainder of this chapter will largely use 'active' forms of citizenship as examples of the main issues in this area.

Digital natives vs. digital immigrants

There is an ongoing debate about 'digital natives vs. digital immigrants' in popular culture, which refers to how familiar two categories of user are with technology and the internet. Broadly, a 'digital native' is described as someone who grew up with the internet, whereas a 'digital immigrant' is typically someone who saw the introduction of the internet within their lifetime (Prensky, 2001). These discussions are often around generational differences, although generational differences in themselves represent a wider debate. Indeed, there are plenty of debates surrounding generational distinctions, particularly when it comes to technology use. Most often these seek to understand generational differences in use, attitudes, competencies, and experiences associated with new technologies (Van Volkom, Stapley, & Amaturo, 2014). This is often referred to as an example of the 'digital divide', in which older adults are compared to young adults and sometimes their middle-aged counterparts. Typically, studies have found that older adults find certain technologies such as mobile phones less user-friendly than young and middle-aged adults (Van Volkom et al., 2014), and younger adults tend to use a wider range of technologies than older adults (Olson, O'Brien, Rogers, & Charness, 2011) and have more positive attitudes towards them (Van der Kaay & Young, 2012). Furthermore, older adults often are slower to adopt new technologies than their younger counterparts (Zickuhr & Madden, 2012). Similar trends seem to exist when exploring generational differences in using certain types of devices or internet functions. For example, young adults tend to engage more in text messaging (Van Volkom, Stapley, & Malter, 2013) and use social networking sites more (Van Volkom et al., 2013) than older adults.

The notion of 'digital natives vs. digital immigrants' has been applied to a range of empirical enquires. Recent research illustrates how digital natives and digital immigrants have different perceptions about technology platforms, which goes some way to explain why some users continue to use certain platforms (Metallo & Agrifoglio, 2015). Interestingly, the notion of 'digital natives vs. digital immigrants' arises in debates about learning approaches, with the suggestion that digital natives learn differently from digital immigrants, particularly with respect to them being more likely to parallel process and multi-task (Prensky, 2001). Despite the popularity of this notion, there is little evidence to support the proposition that so-called digital natives do learn differently from digital immigrants (Kirschner & De Bruyckere, 2017; Rikhye, Cook, & Berge, 2009), leading some researchers to propose the metaphor of a 'digital melting pot', supporting the notion of integrating rather than separating these two groups (Stoerger, 2009). Removing these categorisations also seems important given the fact that evidence shows how older adults can be an important source of support for their peers in using digital media (Hunsaker, Nguyen, Fuchs, Karaoglu, Djukaric, & Hargittai, 2020). However, it appears that part of the challenge in this regard is that they are very rarely asked (Hunsaker et al., 2020), highlighting how these generational categorisations are actually rather damaging to the way learning to use technology can be socially mediated across generations and so-called 'digital divides'.

It would appear therefore that there is little, if any, empirical evidence to support the idea of 'digital natives vs. digital immigrants'. Additionally, there are three pervasive issues that are relevant here. First, irrespective of age or generation, digital skills are learnt through experience of using relevant technologies (Helsper & Eynon, 2010). As such, one's experience of digital technology would appear to be better as a basis for establishing attitudes and competences than simply arbitrary metrics such as age or generational status. Essentially, anyone can become a digital native with the relevant experiences. The second is that these labels are often used synonymously to describe someone's digital competence, yet this is multi-faceted. For example, how would we label someone who is fully capable of using their smartphone but is not yet literate in accessing or using FaceTime on the phone? A single label for someone's level of literacy in using digital technology and aspects of the internet is as meaningless as saying someone is 'classroom literate' to describe their competence in the range of subjects they study at school. The final issue is that within the next few decades, all Westerners will have grown up alongside digital technology and the internet and so digital immigrants will cease to exist. It is perhaps pertinent to dispel this approach altogether given that its long-term future is threatened.

Online vs. offline behaviour

As mentioned in the introduction to this chapter, many debates in cyberpsychology seek to compare online with offline behaviour and, as a result, often treat these as discrete categories. A good example here is that of online vs. offline identities (Hongladarom, 2011), whereby there is an assumption that these identities are categorically discrete and that each one operates entirely unidimensionally, irrespective of the range of contexts that identity may refer to.

When studying online behaviour, a seminal theory in cyberpsychology is that of the *online disinhibition effect* (Suler, 2004). This effect was based on claims that computer-mediated communication (CMC) fosters anonymity, which generates disinhibition (Sproull & Kiesler, 1986). Indeed, according to Sproull and Kiesler:

> People interacting on a computer are isolated from social cues and feel safe
> from surveillance and criticism. This feeling of privacy makes them feel less
> inhibited with others. It also makes it easy for them to disagree with, confront,
> or take exception to others' opinions. (1991: 48–49)

Early research to corroborate this effect includes a comparison of face-to-face
meetings and 'mail-mediated' discussions. This study revealed that the social
status of group members was less impactful on decisions in mail-mediated
discussions than face-to-face ones (Dubrovsky, Kiesler, & Sethna,1991).

The key principles of the online disinhibition effect (Suler, 2004, 2005)
include:

- **Dissociative anonymity** – we can separate ourselves from our 'real'
  identity, therefore there is detachment from our words and actions.
- **Invisibility** – we can be present but not have to reveal our presence (e.g.
  lurking).
- **Asynchronicity** – interactions do not take place in real time, therefore we
  do not see the effects of our words or actions on others.
- **Solipsistic introjection** – a lack of complete information or cues from
  others results in us filling the gaps with an imagined persona.
- **Dissociative imagination** – we are interacting in a fantasy dimension and
  are detached from the responsibilities these actions bring.
- **Minimisation of status and authority** – we have fewer indicators of social
  status online, therefore fear of authority is less.

Two other, more recent factors include:

- **Perceived privacy** – we believe our interactions are private when in fact
  they are able to be accessed by anyone.
- **Social facilitation** – we believe that others deem certain behaviours to be
  acceptable, therefore we are more likely to behave in a similar way.

Research that has sought to test the assertions of this theory include experimental findings from Lapidot-Lefler and Barak (2012). Specifically, they
compared experimental conditions of anonymity vs. no anonymity, visibility
vs. invisibility, and eye-contact vs. lack of eye-contact. Findings showed that
lack of eye-contact was the most influential factor in determining negative
outcomes of online disinhibition, and that anonymity may not in itself be a sufficient condition to determine such effects.

The effects of online disinhibition can be characterised in two ways. First,
they can have a 'benign' effect, whereby disinhibition can provide an opportunity to explore identity and foster diverse experiences. The second – which is
more a part of the cyberpsychology debate – is that of 'toxic' disinhibition,
which results in negative and destructive interactions (Suler, 2005). For
example, evidence suggests that the benign benefits of online disinhibition

include improved self-understanding, resolution of personal conflicts, enhanced socially beneficial behaviours, and increased self-disclosure (Lapidot-Lefler & Barak, 2015; Valkenburg, Schouten, & Peter, 2005). However, toxic disinhibition can result in behaviours such as trolling, flaming, and cyberbullying (Alonzo & Aiken, 2004).

When considering the evidence-base, there is some support for the assertions of this theory. For example, evidence of the effects of anonymity can be observed in the classic social psychology literature, such as how diminished personalised social cues impact on behaviour (Festinger, Pepitone, & Newcomb, 1952). In the case of online settings, anonymity promotes de-individuation and thus generates less favourable behaviour and/or collective action (Cho & Kwon, 2015; Joinson, 2007; Postmes, 2007).

The notion of anonymity when being applied to online settings is a valid one but only to an extent. That is, anonymity online operates on a continuum ranging from being more or less fully anonymous (e.g. lurking or observing) to being identifiable (e.g. social networking sites where we generally use our real name and biographical details). In this sense, the principle of anonymity cannot fully explain disinhibited behaviour in all online settings, given that it is not possible in all online spaces. The same issue applies to invisibility as there are online spaces and types of interactions in which we simply cannot be invisible (e.g. online video-chat). Cyberbullying is a good example of an online behaviour that could be said to be a toxic outcome of online disinhibition, yet contradicts the notion that there is a minimisation of status and power, given that power imbalances form part of the definitional terms of this behaviour (Olweus & Limber, 2018). Therefore, the principles of online disinhibition can go some way to explore human behaviour and its potential variations from 'real-world' behaviour but lack nuance when considering the range of online spaces we occupy. Additionally, there is an assumption that CMC takes place independently from the interactions and relationships we form in the 'real world'. For example, the effects of minimisation of status do not readily apply when you consider CMC as an email exchange or video conference between a line manager and their employee(s). As the status markers still exist from the 'real world' to the online world, there is no dichotomy between the two and therefore one shouldn't assume that different behaviours will be displayed. Certainly, it is the case that our online and 'real-world' experiences are becoming increasingly intertwined (Haythornthwaite & Wellman, 2002). This issue has been thrown into stark relief by the recent Covid-19 pandemic, in which the vast majority of social interactions, together with work and study activities that may have typically occurred in co-located spaces, have been transferred to technologically mediated alternatives (e.g. video-conferencing). In these cases, describing our interaction partners as 'online friends' is not especially meaningful, even though at the time the interactions were probably occurring online only.

In summary, principles such as the online disinhibition effect have indeed been influential within cyberpsychology and certainly have provided a

cornerstone to the CMC literature. However, my view is that these principles desperately need updating, or at the very least require empirical testing
in respect of the different types of online spaces. My expectation would be
that although they may apply in some cases, these theoretical principles
cannot explain all types of behaviour that occur in the range of online
spaces that now exist, and therefore require further scholarly attention and
scrutiny.

Behavioural transfer across contexts

A further issue to consider in the area of online citizenship is the intersection of
our behaviours in online spaces and in the 'real world', and the extent to which
they impact one another. We tend to focus our attention on online behaviour
and how this impacts upon behaviours in the 'real world', although the relationship in many cases is bidirectional. For example, 'offline self-regulation' has
been considered important in how people subsequently wish to present
themselves online (Marder, Houghton, Joinson, & Shankar, 2014). Offline
behaviour can be regulated for the sake of online purposes. An example of this
would be when someone decides to walk or run further than usual because they
are tracking their statistics on Strava (or any other fitness app) and want to
showcase their achievements to their app followers. Conversely, online
behaviour can be regulated for offline purposes. For example, a loyal customer
leaving an overly positive Google or TripAdvisor review for their favourite
local restaurant may not only impact upon that business's reputation but
also the reviewer, perhaps by being offered a discount or 'freebie' during
their next visit.

Behavioural transfer between contexts is clearly a relevant issue in our
everyday experiences of living in a digital society. Perhaps the most prominent
discussion in cyberpsychology on this issue relates to collective action, and
how online settings can promote collectivity which may result in these actions
being realised, often in 'real-world' contexts. This may be underpinned by the
Social Identity Model of Deindividuation Effects (SIDE model; Postmes, 2007;
Spears, Postmes, Lea, & Watt, 2001), which, although not exclusively a theory
to explain online behaviour, is relevant here. The main principle of the SIDE
model is that within a given group, one's personal identity is diminished and
therefore one becomes more anonymous/less identifiable, which can result in
heightened group identity and thus being more prone to follow a collective
agenda or action (Spears et al., 2001). In relation to behavioural transfer
between online and 'real-world' contexts, this model is relevant when we
consider the wide range of online spaces and functionalities which can bring
like-minded people together (e.g. Facebook communities, groups, hashtags,
etc.) where collective identity and strength can be fostered, leading to 'real-
world' behaviours. There are many examples of how 'real-world' collective
action has been motivated by online activism, such as the #MeToo

movement – and perhaps the more recent infamous case of how a former US President's tweets led far-right protesters to attack the Capitol Building in Washington, DC. These effects are not just isolated to socio-political movements of course, but these perhaps are the best examples to illuminate behavioural transfer between contexts.

Conclusion

Returning to the main thrust of this chapter, debates in cyberpsychology have a tendency to compare categories of contexts, such as online vs. offline behaviour, or broad types of citizens, such as 'digital natives vs. digital immigrants' and generational differences. Overall, I observe this to be largely unhelpful in resolving debates in the field, and in the main fails to capture the intricacies of individual-level and context-level interactions which occur through our online citizenship experiences. Although scientific debate has some role in advancing fields of research, when these debates are polarised and sometimes based on popular opinion rather than scientific enquiry, this creates barriers to progress. I certainly see this as being the case for debates around 'digital immigrants' in particular, as it won't be long in Western society when this will no longer be relevant.

Box 4.2: Thinking activity

Think about an example when you operate exclusively online, where there is no transfer of identity or behaviour to the 'real world'. What factors determine your behaviour and how might this be different if there was a 'real-world' component?

Now think of an example where you are part of a group or community and this operates both online and in the 'real world'. How do the behaviours across these contexts interact with one another?

Box 4.3: Take-home message

In a digital society, it is becoming more difficult to categorise ourselves and our behaviours based on whether they are 'online' or 'offline', as these can interact a great deal. It is better to avoid such categorisations and instead explore behaviour itself and how this manifests (perhaps differently) under different conditions and contexts. This will help acknowledge that behaviours do not remain exclusively online or offline, but instead are rather fluid across contexts.

References

Alonzo, M., & Aiken, M. (2004). Flaming in electronic communication. *Decision Support Systems, 36* (3), 205–213. https://doi.org/10.1016/S0167-9236(02)00190-2

Bassett, D. (2018). Digital afterlives: From social media platforms to Thanabots and beyond. In C. Tandy (Ed.), *Death and anti-death, Vol. 16: 200 years after Frankenstein.* Ann Arbor, MI: Ria University Press.

Cho, D., & Kwon, K.H. (2015). The impacts of identity verification and disclosure of social cues on flaming in online user comments. *Computers in Human Behavior, 51,* 363–372. https://doi.org/10.1016/j.chb.2015.04.046

Dubrovsky, V.J., Kiesler, S., & Sethna, B.N. (1991). The equalization phenomenon: Status effects in computer-mediated and face-to-face decision-making groups. *Human-Computer Interaction, 6* (2), 119–146. https://doi.org/10.1207/s15327051hci0602_2

Festinger, L., Pepitone, A., & Newcomb, T. (1952). Some consequences of de-individuation in a group. *Journal of Abnormal and Social Psychology, 47* (2), 382–389. https://doi.org/10.1037/h0057906

Haythornthwaite, C., & Wellman, H. (2002). The Internet in everyday life: An introduction. In B. Wellman & C. Haythornthwaite (Eds.), *The Internet in everyday life* (pp. 3–41). Oxford: Blackwell.

Helsper, E.J., & Eynon, R. (2010). Digital natives: Where is the evidence? *British Educational Research Journal, 36* (3), 503–520. https://doi.org/10.1080/01411920902989227

Hongladarom, S. (2011). Personal identity and the self in the online and offline world. *Minds and Machine, 21,* 533. https://doi.org/10.1007/s11023-011-9255-x

Hunsaker, A., Nguyen, M.H., Fuchs, J., Karaoglu, G., Djukaric, T., & Hargittai, E. (2020). Unsung helpers: Older adults as a source of digital media support for their peers. *The Communication Review, 23* (4), 309–330. https://doi.org/10.1080/10714421.2020.1829307

Joinson, A. (2007). Disinhibition and the Internet. In J. Gackenbach (Ed.), *Psychology and the Internet: Intrapersonal, interpersonal, and transpersonal implications* (pp. 75–92). London: Elsevier.

Kasket, E. (2020). *All the ghosts in the machine: The digital afterlife of your personal data.* London: Robinson.

Kirschner, O.A., & De Bruyckere, P. (2017). The myths of the digital native and the multitasker. *Teaching and Teacher Education, 67,* 135–142. https://doi.org/10.1016/j.tate.2017.06.001

Kirwan, G., & Power, A. (2013). *Cybercrime: The psychology of online offenders.* Cambridge: Cambridge University Press.

Lapidot-Lefler, N., & Barak, A. (2012). Effects of anonymity, invisibility, and lack of eye-contact on toxic online disinhibition. *Computers in Human Behavior, 28* (2), 434–443. https://doi.org/10.1016/j.chb.2011.10.014

Lapidot-Lefler, N., & Barak, A. (2015). The benign online disinhibition effect: Could situational factors induce self-disclosure and prosocial behaviors? *Cyberpsychology: Journal of Psychosocial Research on Cyberspace, 9* (2), 3. https://doi.org/10.5817/CP2015-2-3

Marder, B., Houghton, D., Joinson, A., & Shankar, A. (2014). An investigation into self-regulation offline associated with multiple audiences present on Facebook. Abstract presentation at the *European Association of Social Psychology General Meeting 2014,* Amsterdam, Netherlands.

Metallo, C., & Agrifoglio, R. (2015). The effects of generational differences on use continuance of Twitter: An investigation of digital natives and digital immigrants. *Behaviour and Information Technology*, *34* (9), 869–881. https://doi.org/10.1080/0144929X.2015.1046928

Olson, K.E., O'Brien, M.A., Rogers, W.A., & Charness, N. (2011). Diffusion of technology: Frequency of use for younger and older adults. *Ageing International*, *36*, 123–145. https://doi.org/10.1007/s12126-010-9077-9

Olweus, D., & Limber, S.P. (2018). Some problems with cyberbullying research. *Current Opinion in Psychology*, *19*, 139–143. https://doi.org/10.1016/j.copsyc.2017.04.012

Postmes, T. (2007). The psychological dimensions of collective action, online. In A. Joinson, K. McKenna, T. Postmes, & U. Reips (Eds.), *The Oxford handbook of Internet psychology* (pp. 165–184). Oxford: Oxford University Press.

Prensky, M. (2001). Digital natives, digital immigrants Part 1. *On the Horizon*, *9* (5), 1–6. https://doi.org/10.1108/10748120110424816

Rikhye, R., Cook, S., & Berge, Z.L. (2009). Digital natives vs. digital immigrants: Myth or reality? *International Journal of Instructional Technology and Distance Learning*, *6* (2), 3–10. https://itdl.org/Journal/Feb_09/article01.htm

Rydell, R.J., & Boucher, K.L. (2010). Capitalizing on multiple social identities to prevent stereotype threat: The moderating role of self-esteem. *Personality and Social Psychology Bulletin*, *36* (2), 239–250. https://doi.org/10.1177/0146167209355062

Rydell, R.J., McConnell, A.R., & Beilock, S.L. (2009). Multiple social identities and stereotype threat: Imbalance, accessibility, and working memory. *Journal of Personality and Social Psychology*, *96* (5), 949–966. https://doi.org/10.1037/a0014846

Shaw, H., Ellis, D.A., & Ziegler, F.V. (2018). The Technology Integration Model (TIM): Predicting the continued use of technology. *Computers in Human Behavior*, *83*, 204–214. https://doi.org/10.1016/j.chb.2018.02.001

Spears, R., Postmes, T., Lea, M., & Watt, S.E. (2001). A SIDE view of social influence. In J.P. Forgas & K.D. Williams (Eds.), *Social influence: Direct and indirect processes* (pp. 331–350). Hove: Psychology Press.

Sproull, L., & Kiesler, S. (1986). Reducing social context cues: Electronic mail in organizational communication. *Management Science*, *32* (11), 1492–1512. https://doi.org/10.1287/mnsc.32.11.1492

Sproull, L., & Kiesler, S. (1991). *Connections: New ways of working in the networked organization*. Cambridge, MA: MIT Press.

Stoerger, S. (2009). The digital melting pot: Bridging the digital native–immigrant divide. *First Monday*, *14* (7). https://doi.org/10.5210/fm.v14i7.2474

Suler, J. (2004). The online disinhibition effect. *CyberPsychology & Behavior*, *7* (3), 321–326. https://doi.org/10.1089/1094931041291295

Suler, J. (2005). Contemporary media forum: The online disinhibition effect. *International Journal of Applied Psychoanalytic Studies*, *2* (2), 184–188. https://doi.org/10.1002/aps.42

Valkenburg, P.M., Schouten, A.P., & Peter, J. (2005). Adolescents' identity experiments on the Internet. *New Media & Society*, *7* (3), 383–402. https://doi.org/10.1177/1461444805052282

Van der Kaay, C.D., & Young, W. (2012). Age-related differences in technology usage among community college faculty. *Community College Journal of Research and Practice*, *36* (8), 570–579. https://doi.org/10.1080/10668920903054865

Van Volkom, M., Stapley, J.C., & Amaturo, V. (2014). Revisiting the digital divide: Generational differences in technology use in everyday life. *North American Journal of Psychology*, *16* (3), 557–574.

Van Volkom, M., Stapley, J.C., & Malter, J. (2013). Use and perception of technology: Sex and generational differences in a community sample. *Educational Gerontology, 39* (10), 729–740. https://doi.org/10.1080/03601277.2012.756322

Zickuhr, K., & Madden, M. (2012). *Older adults and internet use.* Pew Research Center's Internet and American Life Project. Retrieved 23 July 2020 from: https://www. pewresearch.org/internet/2012/06/06/older-adults-and-internet-use/

5 Screen-time vs. screen use

As we discussed in Chapter 3, the technology use literature is largely disparate and presents little in the way of conceptual clarity or integration. Arguably, a term that is more prevalent than 'technology use' in current academic and societal debate is that of 'screen-time'. Generally, this is used when referring to societal concerns about the effects of spending too much time on screens. The effects perspective will be discussed fully in Chapter 6, however, the current chapter will discuss the conceptual basis of what 'screen-time' actually means. This will be used as a basis from which to argue for the methodological approaches best suited to this area of debate. We see again here the focus on time as the primary metric of interest, once more highlighting the preoccupation with time in the field.

As recently noted, definitions of screen-time vary considerably and this poses a challenge when attempting to synthesise findings from this broad literature (Kaye, Orben, Ellis, Hunter, & Houghton, 2020). For example, the Oxford English Dictionary (2020) defines screen-time as 'time spent using a device such as a computer, television, or games console'. Interestingly, this definition does not make specific mention of smartphones, which arguably take up a significant proportion of our screen-time (What Mobile, 2019). In contrast, the World Health Organization's most recent guidelines focus on the issue of sedentary screen-time and define it as 'time spent passively watching screen-based entertainment (TV, computer, mobile devices). This does not include active screen-based games where physical activity or movement is required' (WHO, 2019: 5). These two definitions go some way to illustrate a key issue in the debate. That is, that there is a tendency to consider screen-time as a unidimensional and homogeneous construct, which seems problematic given the vast array and diversity of lifestyle behaviours which are undertaken via screens. Furthermore, we might ask, why the obsession with time as a metric? From a psychological perspective, this is not especially interesting and provides no scientific value in helping us explain why time on a screen should be psychologically relevant (Aagaard, Steninge, & Zhang, 2021; Orben, 2021). It also tends to be studied in isolation from how 'screen-time' functions in the broader context of what we may correspondingly describe as 'non-screen-time'. Indeed, having a label for 'non-screen-time' is somewhat bizarre and non-descript given the range of everyday activities it would encompass. In my view, the same issue applies to the 'screen-time' label. A further issue is that there is an implicit assumption that any 'screen-time' activity involves visually looking at a screen. However, some device manufacturers obtain data from listening to music or audio within screen-time metrics, which seems a little strange to me. Therefore, even the basic question about what constitutes a 'screen-time' activity, if indeed this considered a valid construct in the first place, appears to be largely open to interpretation.

When turning to the academic research in this field, one would hope for some clarity on this issue. Unfortunately, this is not the case. The current scientific literature presents a broad selection of terms which seem to map on to screen-time in some form or other. These include, but are not restricted to: 'sedentary screen-based behaviour' (Suchert, Hanewinkel, Isensee, & Läuft Study Group, 2015), 'media time' (Stockdale, Coyne, & Padilla-Walker, 2018; Twenge & Campbell, 2019), 'screen time' or 'screen use' (Ferguson, 2017; Houghton, Lawrence, Hunter, Zadow, Rosenberg, Wood et al., 2018; Wu, Tao, Zhang, Zhang, Chen, Yang et al., 2016), 'new media screen time' (Twenge, Joiner, Rogers, & Martin, 2018), 'digital media time' (Twenge & Campbell, 2019), 'technology use' (Nesi & Prinstein, 2015), 'digital engagement' (Orben & Przybylski, 2020), and 'digital technology use' (Orben & Przybylski, 2019). Clearly, this is a significant barrier when attempting to review how so-called 'screen-time' relates to psychological and social impacts.

In an attempt to resolve the issue, a number of researchers have recommended that the term 'screen-time' and what it represents be retired (Aagaard et al., 2021; LSE, 2016, 2017; Orben, 2021), as it does not provide any meaningful insight into the range of uses which screens offer. Indeed, some researchers have proposed that rather than screen-time, we should consider viewing the issue through the lens of the three Cs: content (what is being engaged with), context (how we are interacting with users of media), and child/or user (understanding who the specific users are) (Guernsey, 2014). When seeking to understand the range of psychological impacts screens may hold, this approach certainly has greater utility and potential than time *per se*. This is especially useful when we consider that debates about 'screen-time' are often conflated with social media (e.g. Royal College of Paediatrics and Child Health, 2018).

Taking this further, there is perhaps a distinction to be drawn between 'screen-time' and 'screen use'. That is, researchers seeking to measure *behaviours* (as noted in Chapter 3) may indeed be able to quantify these numerically as 'screen-time', particularly through objective data tracking such as screen-time apps or data logs. This can provide metrics which provide overall screen-time but perhaps more usefully, metrics based on different types of categories of app. For example, the most recent Apple screen-time app provides a numeric breakdown of time spent on one's device based on nine categories of app or website use:

1 Social networking
2 Entertainment
3 Productivity
4 Games
5 Reading and reference

6 Creativity

7 Education

8 Health and fitness

9 Other.

Here, we have an accurate measure of screen-time in which we can capture actual usage and tell us something more specific about types of use.

However, other researchers may seek alternative insights such as subjective experiences associated with screen use or gratifications sought via screen use (see Chapter 3 for an overview of the uses and gratifications perspective). Indeed, these are valid insights, but are perhaps best termed as 'screen uses' rather than 'screen-time' in an attempt to avoid confusion with the aforementioned numerical categorisation of screen-time. Such an approach requires conceptual integration and agreement on the range of uses which may be garnered via screens. Table 5.1 provides a conceptual framework of how this may be achieved by mapping the 'what', the 'how', and the 'why' of screen uses.

As you can see from Table 5.1, each substantive category of use associated with a specific motivation or need is itemised and these comprise a range of indicative behaviours. It is recommended that if researchers want to quantify 'screen-time', they do this by collecting numerical data of constituent behaviours via objective digital traces. However, if they are seeking a broader understanding of 'uses', taking broad categories and using perceptions/attitudes/endorsements associated with these may be more appropriate given the difficulties in accurately quantifying these numerically from the vast array of constituent behaviours.

Table 5.1 hopefully illuminates the fact that 'use' can refer to more than just time spent using technology. It may refer to the underpinning purpose or reason for using a technology. Clearly, there are some categories of use here which are more psychologically interesting than others. The final category, 'utilities', for example – which often is captured in 'screen-time' measures – is not especially interesting to psychologists, highlighting why distinguishing usage in this way is important.

Making use of objective digital traces such as via Apple screen-time apps and server data such as via Google website visits is an area of interest to help identify more accurate and quantifiable behaviours to represent time spent using certain apps, frequency of visits to types of websites, and so on. This might be a truer measure of screen-time behaviours for certain uses and thus be a better way to compare findings. The practicalities and ethics of collecting online data will be discussed in more detail in Chapter 10. However, not all of these necessitate that researchers themselves have primary access to all these behaviours, but rather in some cases (e.g. search histories) ask participants to access this information for a specified time-frame and report back this numeric data. This may provide a suitable compromise between relying on subjective self-reports of estimates and participant privacy.

Table 5.1 Conceptual framework for screen uses ('what'), behaviours ('how'), and categories ('why')

Category of use ('why')	Sub-type	Indicative uses ('what')	Indicative screen-time behaviours (garnered via log data) ('how')
Social	Interactive/ bidirectional	Video/audio calls, instant messaging, texting, emailing	Frequency of video calls/phone calls per week/day, hours/minutes video calls/ phone calls per week/day, frequency of text messages sent/received per week/day
	Broadcasting	Posting own content on social media, blogging, vlogging	Number of posts per week/day
	Reactive	Commenting on posts, 'liking'/'reacting' to content	Activity log data from social media timelines
	Passive	Observing social media content, 'lurking' on discussion boards/Twitter threads	Social networking Apple screen-time app metrics
Educational/ Work		Undertaking digital self-assessments; accessing pre-recorded educational content; accessing digital learning resources (e-books, journals, news articles, software); undertaking written work (writing assignments, writing reports); administrative tasks (submitting work, obtaining feedback, completing spreadsheets)	Hours/minutes per week/day using online library websites, databases, VLEs, etc. from search history, version history analytics from cloud drives on documents, 'Reading and Reference' Apple screen-time metrics
Entertainment		Watching/streaming videos, films, TV; watching pornography; listening to music; solo gaming	Hours/minutes per week/day from screen-time app data relating to video-streaming and music apps, 'Entertainment' Apple screen-time data

Table 5.1 (Continued)

Category of use ('why')	Sub-type	Indicative uses ('what')	Indicative screen-time behaviours (garnered via log data) ('how')
Non-sedentary		Using fitness videos; exergaming; taking part in geo-located gaming	Hours/minutes per week/day using fitness apps from screen-time app logs, 'Health and Fitness' Apple screen-time app metrics
Informational		Using navigational geo-location for travel; using search engines; seeking information on current affairs (news, sport, weather, events, travel); supporting lifestyle activities (cooking recipes, YouTube tutorials, travel reviews, using fitness and health monitoring apps)	Frequency of searches per week/day from search engine history, visits per week/day to certain websites based on search history
Utilities		Using tools (calculator, alarm clock, clock, camera, notes); obtaining goods and services (travel tickets, event booking, online shopping, online banking)	Frequency of app loads per week/day

Conclusion

This chapter has distinguished between screen-time and screen use and made some suggestions about how this could be conceptualised and operationalised within scholarly work. The suggestions in this chapter are especially important given that there is not yet sufficient conceptual clarity or agreement to underpin this. This has grave implications for a rapidly developing field, especially in addressing key societal debates around issues such as the effects of 'screen-time'. The literature on screen-time effects is discussed in Chapter 6 and highlights further the challenges when working in a field which is lacking a solid conceptual basis.

Box 5.1: Thinking activity

What might health policy guidelines look like if we were to take a screen-use rather than a screen-time approach? Provide examples of specific practical guidance points you would recommend using.

Box 5.2: Take-home message

Screen-time does not offer a psychological explanation behind our technology use based on the wide range of experiences they afford us. Despite the prominent focus on time as a metric, from a psychological perspective understanding usage (why we use, what we are using, what purpose is it fulfilling) is a much more interesting line of enquiry. Objective data can allow us accurate insights into screen-time, perhaps unlike subjective reports, but this is only one aspect of a much broader question relating to screen use.

References

Aagaard, J., Steninge, A., & Zhang, Y. (2021). On the hermeneutics of screen time: A qualitative case study of phubbing. *AI and Society*. https://www.springerprofessional.de/en/on-the-hermeneutics-of-screen-time/19147750

Ferguson, C.J. (2017). Everything in moderation: Moderate use of screens is unassociated with child behavior problems. *Psychiatric Quarterly*, *88* (4), 797–805. https://doi.org/10.1007/s11126-016-9486-3

Guernsey, L. (2014). *How the iPad affects young children, and what we can do about it.* TEDxMidAtlantic, video, 27 April.. www.youtube.com/watch?v=P41_nyYY3Zg

Houghton, S., Lawrence, D., Hunter, S.C., Zadow, C., Rosenberg, M., Wood, L. et al. (2018). Reciprocal relationships between trajectories of depressive symptoms and screen media use during adolescence. *Journal of Youth and Adolescence*, *47* (11), 2453–2467. https://doi.org/10.1007/s10964-018-0901-y

Kaye, L.K., Orben, A., Ellis, D.A., Hunter, S.C., & Houghton, S. (2020). The conceptual and methodological mayhem of 'screen-time'. *International Journal of Environmental Research and Public Health, 17* (10), 3661. https://doi.org/10.3390/ijerph17103661

London School of Economics and Political Science (LSE) (2016). *What and how should parents be advised about 'screen time'?* Retrieved 16 April 2020 from: https://blogs.lse.ac.uk/parenting4digitalfuture/2016/07/06/what-and-how-should-parents-be-advised-about-screen-time/

London School of Economics and Political Science (LSE) (2017). *The trouble with 'screen time' rules.* Retrieved 16 April 2020 from: https://blogs.lse.ac.uk/parenting-4digitalfuture/2017/06/08/the-trouble-with-screen-time-rules/

Nesi, J., & Prinstein, M.J. (2015). Using social media for social comparison and feedback-seeking: Gender and popularity moderate associations with depressive symptoms. *Journal of Abnormal Child Psychology, 43* (8), 1427–1438. https://doi.org/10.1007/s10802-015-0020-0

Orben, A. (2021). Digital diet: A 21st century approach to understanding digital technologies and development. *Infant and Child Development*, e2228. https://doi.org/10.1002/icd.2228

Orben, A., & Przybylski, A.K. (2019). The association between adolescent well-being and digital technology use. *Nature Human Behaviour, 3*, 173–182. https://doi.org/10.1038/s41562-018-0506-1

Orben, A., & Przybylski, A.K. (2020). Teenage sleep and technology engagement across the week. *PeerJ, 8*, e8427. https://doi.org/10.7717/peerj.8427

Oxford English Dictionary (OED) (2020). *OED online.* Oxford: Oxford University Press. https://www.oed.com

Royal College of Paediatrics and Child Health (2018). *Impact of social media and screen-use on young people's health.* Retrieved 20 July 2020 from: https://www.rcpch.ac.uk/sites/default/files/2018-05/final_rcpch_response_to_social_media_and_screentime_consultation.pdf

Stockdale, L.A., Coyne, S.M., & Padilla-Walker, L.M. (2018). Parent and child technoference and socioemotional behavioral outcomes: A nationally representative study of 10- to 20-year-old adolescents. *Computers in Human Behavior, 88*, 219–226. https://doi.org/10.1016/j.chb.2018.06.034

Suchert, V., Hanewinkel, R., Isensee, B., & Läuft Study Group (2015). Sedentary behavior, depressed affect, and indicators of mental well-being in adolescence: Does the screen only matter for girls? *Journal of Adolescence, 42*, 50–58. https://doi.org/10.1016/j.adolescence.2015.03.014

Twenge, J.M., & Campbell, W.K. (2019). Media use is linked to lower psychological well-being: Evidence from three datasets. *Psychiatric Quarterly, 90* (2), 311–331. https://doi.org/10.1007/s11126-019-09630-7

Twenge, J.M., Joiner, T.E., Rogers, M.L., & Martin, G.N. (2018). Increases in depressive symptoms, suicide-related outcomes and suicide rates among US adolescents after 2010 and links to increased new media screen time. *Clinical Psychological Science, 6* (1), 3–17. https://doi.org/10.1177/2167702617723376

What Mobile (2019). *UK's screen time stats revealed.* Retrieved 20 July 2020 from: https://www.whatmobile.net/Opinion/article/uks-screen-time-stats-revealed

World Health Organization (WHO) (2019). *Guidelines on physical activity, sedentary behaviour and sleep for children under 5 years of age.* Geneva: WHO. https://apps.who.int/iris/handle/10665/311664. License: CC BY-NC-SA 3.0 IGO.

Wu, X., Tao, S., Zhang, S., Zhang, Y., Chen, K., Yang, Y. et al. (2016). Impact of screen time on mental health problems progression in youth: A 1-year follow-up study. *BMJ Open, 6* (11), e011533. https://doi.org/10.1136/bmjopen-2016-011533

PART 3

Effects

6 Screen-time effects

Box 6.1: Current questions

- How much is too much screen-time?
- Is screen-time bad for our physical health?
- How does screen-time relate to mental health?

One of the most prominent public debates of the twenty-first century is that of 'screen-time' and its effects in particular on young people. Indeed, this issue is widely represented in mainstream media and in health policy, which has driven a plethora of research enquiry from a broad range of stakeholders including psychologists, psychiatrists, social workers, and paediatricians. Whilst being of great interest, it also remains a hotly debated and controversial issue. The next sections provide a review of the main effects which have been discussed in relation to 'screen-time'.

Health and physical outcomes

Probably the most compelling case about the (negative) outcomes of 'screen-time' is that of physical health correlates. The term 'compelling' here is used in relative terms to that of other theoretical arguments on 'screen-time' and impacts. The main thrust of this issue derives from the fact that time spent using screens is most typically time that might otherwise have been devoted to engaging in non-sedentary activities (e.g. exercise, physical activity). This notion makes conceptual sense and it is the case that in most cases there will be a displacement effect (notwithstanding any specific effects which may be associated with the three Cs of content, context, and 'child', as noted in Chapter 5). This has indeed been found to be the case across some studies. For example, research examining computer use has found that those who use computers the most tend to be less active than those who use them less (Fotheringham, Wonnacott, & Owen, 2000). Similarly, research has found that TV viewing and computer use correlate with amount of sitting/sedentary time (Busschaert, Ridgers, De Bourdeaudhuij, Cardon, Van Cauwenberg, & De Cocker, 2016; Young, Sidell, Koebnick, Saksvig, Mohan, Cohen et al., 2019). Taking this further, research has found that owning a computer and smartphone use are positively related to body mass index (BMI; Lajunen, Keski-Rahkonen, Pulkkinen, Rose, Rissanen, & Kaprio, 2007).

Interestingly, however, some research has not corroborated this effect. For example, recent work suggests minimal evidence that screen-time on smartphones is negatively related to physical health outcomes (Shaw, Ellis, Geyer, Davidson, Ziegler, & Smith, 2020). That is, smartphone daily screen-time and number of pick-ups were found not to be negatively associated with BMI, thereby highlighting the inverse correlation to what may be expected based on the displacement perspective. Also, one study showed there to be no significant long-term impacts of 'screen-time' on changes to physical activity (Gunnell, Flament, Buchholz, Henderson, Obeid, Schubert et al., 2016). Furthermore, smartphone use, video gaming, and internet use were reported not to have a significant impact on BMI or body weight (Jackson, von Eye, Fitzgerald, Witt, & Zhao, 2011). These disparate findings in the literature may be explained in a number of ways, but most noteworthy perhaps is the fact that certain technologies such as smartphones are mobile and therefore do not necessitate sedentary behaviour during use. In the case of smartphones, which have ubiquitous uses (Fullwood, Quinn, Kaye, & Redding, 2017), it is likely that a proportion of their usage is devoted to non-sedentary activities such as tracking fitness or geo-located activity (Kaye & Levy, 2017). Thus, the relationship between 'screen-time' and physical activity is by no means linear, highlighting the need to distinguish between categories of use as outlined in Chapter 5.

As well as issues related to physical activity and health outcomes, there is the matter of sleep behaviour – specifically, that 'screen-time' may be related to poorer sleep, both in terms of quality and quantity (Hale & Guan, 2015). The issue of sleep quantity aligns with the previous discussion about displacement. That is, if someone is using screens when they should be asleep, then this will undoubtedly result in displaced sleep time and therefore shorter sleep duration. In line with this, there is evidence that electronic media use in bed before sleep is negatively related to sleep duration (Lemola, Perkinson-Gloor, Brand, Dewald-Kaufmann, & Grob, 2015). Similarly, using smartphones 'after lights out' has been found to be related to tiredness (Saling & Haire, 2016), and smartphone overuse with unhealthy sleep patterns and insomnia (Tamura, Nishida, Tsuji, & Sakakibara, 2017).

The issue of sleep quality is slightly different. This is often discussed in relation to the biological or physiological impacts associated with screen use. Physiological impacts may include increased arousal and neuroendocrine responses, which may derive from certain types of screen use such as video games (Ivarsson, Anderson, Akerstedt, & Lindblad, 2009; King, Gradisar, Drummond, Lovato, Wessel, Micic et al., 2013). Biological impacts may come from electromagnetic radiation emitted from certain devices such as smartphones, which may delay melatonin production and interfere with sleep onset (Wood, Loughran, & Stough, 2006).

Notwithstanding any health outcomes associated with 'screen-time', additional (positive) outcomes can occur concurrently. For example, whilst sedentary or night-time use of screens may to some extent be associated with poorer health outcomes, the specific uses of screens during this time may be bringing about a range of other psychological or social experiences.

Additionally, the issue of displaced physical activity from screens should be considered in the wider context of other sedentary pursuits such as reading, knitting, or doing jigsaws. Arguably these pursuits also displace time away from physical activity, yet are not often discussed as a public health concern in the way using screens is.

In summary, although the case for displacement in explaining why 'screen-time' relates to various physical health correlates does make some conceptual sense, the evidence is mixed. A wider perspective is warranted regarding how screen use, as a significant public health issue, is qualitatively different from other sedentary pursuits which people engage in in their everyday lives. In respect of practical recommendations, this may only be achieved if various categories of screen use are recognised rather than assuming physical (and psychological) effects are consistent across screen-time more generically.

Psychological functioning

Moving away from physical effects, the most controversial of the 'screen-time' effects debates relates to psychological and social functioning. This debate has tended to focus on aspects of well-being such as depression, anxiety, loneliness, psychological distress, suicide ideation, and psychological well-being (for a recent review, see Ferguson, Kaye, Branley-Bell, Markey, Ivory, Klisinan et al., in press). Whilst some research routinely shows the negative impacts of 'screen-time' or its constituents on psychological functioning (e.g. Twenge, 2019; Twenge & Campbell, 2018), other work has highlighted that the evidence base is far too mixed to conclude any consistent impacts (Odgers & Jensen, 2020; Orben, 2020) or that such effects exist at all (Vuorre, Orben, & Przybylski, 2021). In addition, it has been argued that even in cases where there are observed relationships between 'screen-time' and outcomes, these are usually small in size, and there no convincing longitudinal evidence of causality in these effects (Jensen, George, Russell, & Odgers, 2019; Orben, Dienlin, & Przybylski, 2019; Orben & Przybylski, 2019). Furthermore, covariates tend to explain more when predicting effects than simply 'screen-time' itself (Orben et al., 2019).

To add further to this debate, recent evidence highlights that reported effect sizes between 'screen-time' and psychological functioning are likely to be inflated based on choice of measurements (Shaw et al., 2020). That is, using problematic smartphone use scales appears to inflate the associations with psychological distress symptomology relative to subjective estimates and objective log data. Shaw et al. also found that while problematic smartphone use scales significantly predicted psychological outcomes, objective log data and subjective estimates did not.

This brings us to the theoretical explanations for how or why 'screen-time' should be related to psychosocial functioning. The displacement perspective can only make conceptual sense for some specific types of outcomes and only when we can understand the specific uses of screens. In Chapter 5 we noted there to be various uses of screens, including for entertainment, social use, and information. Social uses may inherently relate to one's perceptions of loneliness (perhaps reduced loneliness in this case) and therefore time spent engaging in other uses may be seen as time taken away from social uses and therefore impact detrimentally on loneliness. There is some theoretical merit in this line of thought, but regrettably much of the 'screen-time' effects research does not seek to understand the various screen uses and therefore it is not clear how or why time on screens as such would theoretically relate to the range of psychosocial outcomes noted in the literature. Recent commentary on this issue noted that one avenue for future research in this area may be to measure the various proportionalities of different types of screen use and how these combinations may draw out differential well-being impacts (Kaye, Orben, Ellis, Hunter, & Houghton, 2020).

Another major issue with the 'screen-time' effects literature is a general absence of thought about how time spent on screens functions within the wider context of everyday life. Taking measurements of time using screens to correlate with physical and psychological variables can only provide a partial explanation about how screens function in the wider context of daily life and what the range of contributors to one's physical and psychological well-being may be.

A related issue is that if we continue to use the term 'screen-time', then, by definition, any activity in which we are not using screens is 'non-screen-time', which is a rather ridiculous notion. Categorising behaviours based on the presence or absence of a screen seems a strange way to conceptualise contemporary human behaviour. Some researchers may want to go even further and propose 'screen-time' vs. 'green time', in which more time spent on screens means less time out in nature, which is suggested to impact detrimentally on well-being (Oswald, Rumbold, Kedzior, & Moore, 2020). As noted in Chapter 5, understanding the affordances which screens provide to fulfil certain uses, rather than focusing on screen-time as a behaviour in itself, is a more useful way forward in this regard. This further assists us in conceptualising how the various ways we use screens affect mental and physical health.

Conclusion

The current scientific understanding of the range of effects associated with screen use is rather limited. This is largely because the field has been too focused on time as the metric of interest. I would argue this is neither interesting nor insightful in forming psychological questions. As outlined in Chapter 5, moving a focus to 'use' would be substantially more interesting and provide greater explanatory value in theorising about the likely effects of screens. Furthermore, this should be considered alongside everyday behaviours which transfer across contexts, so that we do not treat 'screens' as the central focus of enquiry.

> **Box 6.2: Thinking activity**
>
> When thinking about either physical or psychological health outcomes, what might be considered a good mix of various screen uses to help promote healthy functioning? (See Table 5.1 for a list of screen uses.)

> **Box 6.3: Take-home message**
>
> Given the somewhat obsessional focus of time as a metric in this field, we have rather limited understanding of the range of effects associated with how we use screens for a variety of purposes. Moving away from the metric of 'time' to instead consider 'use' (as per Chapter 5) would be substantially more interesting and provide greater explanatory value in theorising about the likely effects.

References

Busschaert, C., Ridgers, N.D., De Bourdeaudhuij, I., Cardon, G., Van Cauwenberg, J., & De Cocker, K. (2016). Socio-demographic, social-cognitive, health-related and physical environmental variables associated with context-specific sitting time in Belgian adolescents: A one-year follow-up study. *PLoS One, 11* (12), e0167553. https://doi.org/10.1371/journal.pone.0167553

Ferguson, C.J., Kaye, L.K., Branley-Bell, D., Markey, P., Ivory, J.D., Klisinan, D. et al. (in press). Like this meta-analysis: Screen media and mental health. *Professional Psychology: Research and Practice.*

Fotheringham, M.J., Wonnacott, R.L., & Owen, N. (2000). Computer use and physical inactivity in young adults: Public health perils and potentials of new information technologies. *Annals of Behavioral Medicine, 22* (4), 269–275. https://doi.org/10.1007/BF02895662

Fullwood, C., Quinn, S., Kaye, L.K., & Redding, C. (2017). My Virtual friend: A qualitative analysis of the attitudes and experiences of Smartphone users: Implications for Smartphone attachment. *Computers in Human Behavior, 75*, 347–355. https://doi.org/10.1016/j.chb.2017.05.029

Gunnell, K.E., Flament, M.F., Buchholz, A., Henderson, K.A., Obeid, N., Schubert, N. et al. (2016). Examining the bidirectional relationship between physical activity, screen time, and symptoms of anxiety and depression over time during adolescence. *Preventive Medicine, 88*, 147–152. https://doi.org/10.1016/j.ypmed.2016.04.002

Hale, L., & Guan, S. (2015). Screen time and sleep among school-aged children and adolescents: A systematic literature review. *Sleep Medicine Reviews, 21*, 50–58. https://doi.org/10.1016/j.smrv.2014.07.007

Ivarsson, M., Anderson, M., Akerstedt, T., & Lindblad, F. (2009). Playing a violent television game affects heart rate variability. *Acta Paediatrica, 98* (1), 166–172. https://doi.org/10.1111/j.1651-2227.2008.01096.x

Jackson, L.A., von Eye, A., Fitzgerald, H.E., Witt, E.A., & Zhao, Y. (2011). Internet use, videogame playing and cell phone use as predictors of children's body mass index (BMI), body weight, academic performance, and social and overall self-esteem. *Computers in Human Behavior, 27* (1), 599–604. https://doi.org/10.1016/j.chb.2010.10.019

Jensen, M., George, M.J., Russell, M.R., & Odgers, C.L. (2019). Young adolescents' digital technology use and mental health symptoms: Little evidence of longitudinal or daily linkages. *Clinical Psychological Science, 7* (6), 1416–1433. https://doi.org/10.1177/2167702619859336

Kaye, L.K., & Levy, A.R. (2017). Reconceptualising the link between screen-time when gaming with physical activity and sedentary behaviour. *Cyberpsychology, Behavior and Social Networking, 20* (12), 769–773. https://doi.org/10.1089/cyber.2017.0067

Kaye, L.K., Orben, A., Ellis, D.A., Hunter, S.C., & Houghton, S. (2020). The conceptual and methodological mayhem of 'screen-time'. *International Journal of Environmental Research and Public Health, 17* (10), 3661. https://doi.org/10.3390/ijerph17103661

King, D.L., Gradisar, M., Drummond, A., Lovato, N., Wessel, J., Micic, G. et al. (2013). The impact of prolonged violent videogaming on adolescent sleep: An experimental study. *Journal of Sleep Research, 22* (2), 137–143. https://doi.org/10.1111/j.1365-2869.2012.01060.x

Lajunen, H.-R., Keski-Rahkonen, A., Pulkkinen, L., Rose, R.J., Rissanen, A., & Kaprio, J. (2007). Are computer and cell phone use associated with body mass index and over-weight? A population study among twin adolescents. *BMC Public Health, 7* (24). https://doi.org/10.1186/1471-2458-7-24

Lemola, S., Perkinson-Gloor, N., Brand, S., Dewald-Kaufmann, J.F., & Grob, A. (2015). Adolescents' electronic media use at night, sleep disturbance, and depressive symptoms in the smartphone age. *Journal of Youth and Adolescence, 44* (2), 405–418. https://doi.org/10.1007/s10964-014-0176-x

Odgers, C.L., & Jensen, M.R. (2020). Annual research review: Adolescent mental health in the digital age: Facts, fears, and future directions. *Journal of Child Psychology and Psychiatry, 61* (3), 336–348. https://doi.org/10.1111/jcpp.13190

Orben, A. (2020). Teenagers, screens and social media: A narrative review of reviews and key studies. *Social Psychiatry and Psychiatric Epidemiology, 55*, 407–414. https://doi.org/10.1007/s00127-019-01825-4

Orben, A., Dienlin, T., & Przybylski, A.K. (2019). Social media's enduring effect on adolescent life satisfaction. *Proceedings of the National Academy of Sciences USA, 116* (21), 10226–10228. https://doi.org/10.1073/pnas.1902058116

Orben, A., & Przybylski, A.K. (2019). The association between adolescent well-being and digital technology use. *Nature Human Behaviour, 3*, 173–182. https://doi.org/10.1038/s41562-018-0506-1

Oswald, T.K., Rumbold, A.R., Kedzior, S.G.E., & Moore, V.M. (2020). Psychological impacts of 'screen time' and 'green time' for children and adolescents: A systematic scoping review. *PLoS One, 15* (9), e0237725. https://doi.org/10.1371/journal.pone.0237725

Saling, L.L., & Haire, M. (2016). Are you awake? mobile phone use after lights out. *Computers in Human Behavior, 64*, 932–937. https://doi.org/10.1016/j.chb.2016.08.006

Shaw, H., Ellis, D.A., Geyer, K., Davidson, B.I., Ziegler, F.V., & Smith, A. (2020). Quantifying smartphone 'use': Choice of measurement impacts relationships between 'usage' and health. *Technology, Mind & Behavior, 1* (2). https://doi.org/10.1037/tmb0000022

Tamura, H., Nishida, T., Tsuji, A., & Sakakibara, H. (2017). Association between excessive use of mobile phone and insomnia and depression among Japanese adolescents.

International Journal of Environmental Research and Public Health, 14 (7), 701. https://doi.org/10.3390/ijerph14070701

Twenge, J.M. (2019). More time on technology, less happiness? Associations between digital-media use and psychological well-being. *Current Directions in Psychological Science, 28* (4), 372–379. https://doi.org/10.1177/0963721419838244

Twenge, J.M., & Campbell, W.K. (2018). Associations between screen time and lower psychological well-being among children and adolescents: Evidence from a population-based study. *Preventive Medicine Reports, 12*, 271–283. https://doi.org/10.1016/j.pmedr.2018.10.003

Vuorre, M., Orben, A., & Przybylski, A.K. (2021). There is no evidence that associations between adolescents' digital technology engagement and mental health problems have increased. *Clinical Psychological Science.* https://doi.org/10.1177/2167702621994549

Wood, A.W., Loughran, S.P., & Stough, C. (2006). Does evening exposure to mobile phone radiation affect subsequent melatonin production? *International Journal of Radiation Biology, 82* (2), 69–76. https://doi.org/10.1080/09553000600599775

Young, D.R., Sidell, M.A., Koebnick, C., Saksvig, B.I., Mohan, Y., Cohen, D.A. et al. (2019). Longitudinal sedentary time among females aged 17 to 23 years. *American Journal of Preventive Medicine, 56* (4), 540–547. https://doi.org/10.1016/j.amepre.2018.11.021

7 Social media and relationships

Box 7.1: Current questions

- Are online friends 'real' friends?
- Can we have good quality relationships online?
- Is social media making us antisocial?

Social media is a broad category that refers to any website or application which enables users to create and share content, or to participate in social networking. Social networking sites (SNSs) such as Facebook, Twitter, TikTok, Instagram, and SnapChat are popular forms of social media that serve personal networking functions as well as being commonly used by organisations for commercial or professional purposes. The focus of this chapter is largely on personal uses of social media, particularly relating to how individuals use these to connect to friends, maintain relationships, and interact and communicate within these networks.

'Personal use' of social media covers a diverse range of experiences. Even within a single social media platform, one's networks can include many types of contacts, including close friends, colleagues, family members, partners, former school friends, and professional contacts. These clearly represent relationships which vary in intimacy, closeness, and familiarity, all of which will have varying impacts on how social media functions for relationship richness and maintenance. This 'context collapse' (multiple audiences in a single context; Davis & Jurgenson, 2014) means that for any given user on a specific social media site, they may be simultaneously managing various 'audiences' in their self-expressions, raising issues for navigating self-presentation behaviours (Davidson & Joinson, 2021; Hogan, 2010; Marwick & Boyd, 2011). This can bring challenges to managing effective interpersonal relations and perceptions, which may explain why some social media interactions/disclosures may seem superficial (Vitak, 2012). The more diverse an audience, the more the user may be obliged to share content which meets the interest of the many, rather than richness for the few. Although it is often assumed that people will work to the principle of the 'lowest common denominator effect' (LCDE), where they constrain their expressions to their strictest audience, other work has suggested that it is the strongest audience which is most influential (Marder, Joinson, Shankar, & Thirlaway, 2016). The 'strongest audience effect' refers to a combination of the standards and values (economical/social) attributed to specific audience members. There has been discussion of the way online behaviours such as those on social media relate to self-presentational efforts and how these feed into interpersonal perceptions (Darbyshire, Kirk, Wall, & Kaye, 2016; Wall, Kaye, & Malone, 2016). Largely, this research suggests that these varying self-presentational disclosures influence the way we relate to and understand one another, highlighting how context collapse on social media may in some cases be detrimental for relationships that are maintained there (particularly those which are online-exclusive). When exploring self-presentational attempts on social media, several key issues have been noted, including permanency of content, public vs. private/protected account, and professional vs. personal/social use (Davidson & Joinson, 2021), all of which will have specific platform affordances.

We also have to consider at what point social media is introduced within relationship formation and maintenance. That is, in some cases, existing contacts may extend their contexts for connection by adding each other to their social media accounts. Conversely, other people may initially meet via social media (or other online platforms such as online dating), initiating the relationship formation process. In this case, there are distinctions to be made about the way social media functions for connecting with others and relationship maintenance. Romantic relationships are of interest here, in that social media has the potential to make visible some key signals in relationship maintenance or breakdown, such as relationship status ('In a relationship with …'), cheating (e.g. private intimate messages to other people), or stalking ('X has requested to follow you').

Certainly over the last few decades, the use of social media and other online platforms for meeting others has grown substantially. Alongside this, online dating has become more accepted in society and is vastly becoming one of the most popular ways to form new relationships, which often includes seeking long-term partners (Anderson, Vogels, & Turner, 2020). One of the benefits of platforms such as social media and online dating is that it is often much easier to see people's preferences and interests to judge whether they might be compatible. This may be important, as homophily is noted to lead to greater relationship stability (Buss, 1985), although this may vary based on the type of partner being sought (short or long term), the gender of the 'seeker' (Jonason & Antoon, 2019), and what categories are being compared for compatibility (Fox-Hamilton, Fullwood, & Kirwan, 2015). That is, in respect of personality matching, research highlights that homophily between traits in partners is not always optimal in determining perceived attraction, especially for openness and conscientiousness (Fox-Hamilton et al., 2015). However, it is certainly the case that online platforms have greater efficacy to make visible people's interests and preferences in the initial contact stages of relationship formation compared with 'real-world' equivalents. As such, people can be more equipped with relevant cues to judge whether they wish to pursue further contact or interaction with a specific target.

The poor relation?

Whether we are referring to online dating or social media platforms, a key debate is the extent to which 'online friends' are equivalent to 'real-world' friends, and how this relates to social ties and relationship quality (Nabi, Prestin, & So, 2013). Some research suggests that 'online friends' cannot be considered to be equivalent to 'real-world' friends given that there are key differences between the two (Cockling & Matthews, 2000; Fröding & Peterson, 2012). With online friends it is argued, there is an absence of spatial space, no involuntary (non-verbal) self-disclosures, and that they do not meet the parameters of 'true' friendship (Cockling & Matthews, 2000). However, others suggest that because we often disclose more online than offline, this leads to stronger relationships in these spaces (Briggle, 2008). Bargh, McKenna, and Fitzsimons (2002) highlight that these sorts of self-disclosures also may encourage online friendships to transfer to the real world. This highlights an issue of critical importance: debates in the field tend to assume online and offline friends are exclusive networks, when in reality there are often significant crossovers between the two (e.g. Cummings, Sproull, & Kiesler, 2002; Snodgrass, Lacy, Dengah, & Fagan, 2011). For example, WhatsApp groups tend to comprise people who we know in the real world, and our Facebook friends are often family members, real-world friends, and colleagues. When using the term 'online' friends, we tend to overlook the fact that our relationship networks are not mutually exclusive between different contexts. This presents conceptual problems when exploring questions such as 'how does time spent with online versus offline friends relate to well-being?', 'are online friends superficial?', and so on. Unfortunately, much of the current conceptual work on this tends to assume exclusivity between online and offline friends. For example, as a pioneering theorist on social network size and stability of relationships, Dunbar (2010) has sought to understand the principles of this to categories of 'online' and 'offline' networking groups, with little acknowledgement of the crossover effects. Dunbar (2016) also makes a pertinent point about the categories we use to consider 'friends' in online contexts and how this may include all network partners rather than distinguishing between 'friends' and 'acquaintances', for example, as in the real world. Arguably, the way we categorise our relationships and the extent to which we consider these as 'friendships' is likely to vary across the different online spaces we use. Facebook uses the term 'friend' to denote one's network partners but this captures a broad range of relationships for any given user (family, friends, colleagues) and many of these partners would not in 'real-world' terms usually fit this sematic category. Perhaps this is one of the reasons we tend to assume this unidimensional categorisation for our 'online friends'.

Theoretical considerations

So, what does the current cyberpsychology literature tell us about how 'online' relationships vary from 'real-world' ones and how this is important to understand our social experiences? Much of the historical debate on this issue has been concerned with the idea that spending time on the internet is problematic for relationships, as this means spending less time engaging with our 'real-world' friends. Indeed, this is supported by the displacement hypothesis (Neuman, 1988; Valkenburg & Peter, 2009), which posits that it is this displacement of time from good quality, meaningful relationships that has a negative effect on the quality of our relationships, impacting detrimentally on our well-being. However, more recent debate has moved beyond this to illuminate that domains on the internet can allow an additional context to socialise (e.g. SNSs), enriching the time we can spend with our friends, and thus enhancing relationship quality and well-being (Ellison, Steinfield, & Lampe, 2007; Kaye & Quinn, 2020). Of course, a critical issue to consider here is whether people are indeed 'being social' on the internet or even on SNSs. Addressing this might help to resolve which of these hypotheses may be most relevant. This leads to the question: 'how social is social media?'

How social is social media?

When posing this question, there are a number of key considerations. One pertinent issue is how people actually engage in different types of interactions with others via social media. When referring to CMC, there may be great diversity in the level of interactions people have with one another based on the types of features they use, which is often reliant on the affordances of both the hardware and software. This is discussed by Meier and Reinecke (2020), who conducted a conceptual review of the extent to which CMC can be considered 'channel-centred' vs. 'communication-centred'. The former can relate to hardware, such as how people interact with the devices themselves, or software, such as the types of social media apps they may use. The latter is at a more intricate level, involving the modalities of communication and network structures (Meier & Reinecke, 2020). These are important distinctions to make when theorising about interactions and relationships via social media, and are pertinent to studying differential outcomes for relationship quality, strength, social ties, and other relevant social affordances. Indeed, a recent review of these issues notes that social connectedness, social capital, and other associated psychosocial constructs are important to consider when theorising how 'social' social media is (Ryan, Allen, Gray, & McInerney, 2017).

When thinking about socialising on social media, we often think about the way people engage in chats, respond to posts, and so on. This has been considered to comprise two types of use: 'active' and 'passive' (Pagani, Hofacker, & Goldsmith, 2011; Shim, Lee, & Park, 2008; Wang, Gaskin, Rost, & Gentile, 2018; Yu, 2016). Active use largely covers any type of behavioural engagement with a social media platform such as posting updates, interacting with others, and so on, whereas passive use involves observing or browsing others' content. However, some researchers now believe these are not particularly useful concepts, especially as use can vary based on posts and sender (Valkenburg, van

Driel, & Beyens, 2021). As such, 'active' use is somewhat vague and it is likely the case that there are various ways we can be 'social' under this category of use. Rafaeli's (1988) work on interactivity is pertinent here, which distinguishes between different levels of responsiveness between communication partners, which is said to range from two-way interactive, to two-way reactive, to one-way non-interactive communication (e.g. browsing). Recent work building on these principles has shown that 'active' use is perhaps a latent variable, in that there are two observable active forms of social media use: interactive (with others) and reactive (to others) (Meier & Reinecke, 2020; Shaw, Pennington, Ngombe, Kessler, & Kaye, 2021). Meier and Reinecke (2020) outline three types of social media use: interactive, reactive, and passive. These vary in respect of the level of interactivity (as per Rafaeli), in that interactive and reactive social media use involve two-way communication between users but interactive is more truly bidirectional and/or synchronous than reactive. Reactive use refers to behaviours in which the user reacts *to* other users rather that interacting *with* them. However, both consist of some level of behavioural engagement between users. On the other hand, passive use (of others) consists of one-way non-interactive behaviour in which the user is an audience/recipient who does not engage behaviourally with others.

The extent to which someone may be considered 'social' on social media, therefore, is perhaps best understood in terms of whether they engage in a range of behaviours that may be deemed to vary in their level of interactivity. This is not to say there is a fixed typology of users, but rather users may vary based on the behaviours which occur in specific contexts/platforms and circumstances. Taking a platform-specific focus here is helpful, and using approaches such as 'social network analysis' can help establish the level of 'socialness' in a given person's network (Hoang, Lim, Achananuparp, Jiang, & Teow, 2011; Meske, Junglas, Schneider, & Jaakonmäki, 2019).

Having conceptual clarity on what being 'social' means on social media can therefore go some way to help us understand more about the relationships that are formed and maintained there, as well as the level of closeness in networks (Sutcliffe, Binder, & Dunbar, 2018). There are a range of theoretical perspectives we can draw on to explore how these varying social media experiences can be considered relationships. One of these is social capital theory (Putnam, 2000), which discusses the social resources that we derive from different types of 'strong ties' and 'weak ties' with others. Our 'strong ties' may be forged from *bonding capital* with individuals who are our close friends or family members. In contrast, our 'weak ties' may derive from *bridging capital* with those in our peripheral or extended networks. Psychologically, we know that both bonding and bridging capital are important, particularly for self-esteem, life satisfaction, and good health (Bargh et al., 2002; De Silva, McKenzie, Harpham, & Huttly, 2005; Helliwell & Putnam, 2004; Stanton-Salazar & Dornbusch, 1995). The benefit of many online platforms is the ability to both connect within our own networks (i.e. with our strong ties) while also connecting across peripheral networks to capitalise on the weaker ties (Selim, Scott, & Kaye, 2021). In this sense, many social media platforms can allow a combination of both bonding and bridging capital, often simultaneously, which is quite unique to the way we situate our relationships with people in different networks in the 'real world'. For example, we do not usually share the same space with our colleagues and family members simultaneously.

The ability of social media to manage multiple networks, relationships, and sub-communities while useful can also be challenging, particularly in terms of what appropriate behaviours to engage in when crossing social boundaries. Take someone who is both a football fan and a churchgoer, for example. They may have friends/followers of these two networks on a given social media site, making it difficult to know what types of behaviours (what information to share, content they interact with, etc.) will be relevant and appropriate for both networks. This makes it quite challenging to maintain effective relationships with the respective networks. There are, of course, opportunities for cross-fertilisation of networks, which is much less likely in the way we physically situate our networks in the 'real world'.

Of course, some social media platforms allow people the opportunity to join sub-communities such as groups, lists, pages, and so on. This offers ways of extending our networks or what we may often call 'weak ties' to those in the wider community who may share similar interests. The potential to develop and maintain relationships in these communities is high given that the content and social norms of these networks are likely to be salient to most, if not all, members. From a theoretical perspective, one way of understanding relation-ships within these sorts of communities is to apply social identity theory (Tajfel, 1978, 1979; Tajfel & Turner, 1979). Social identity theory posits that we define ourselves based on our group membership – namely, that our sense of self moves from the personal (e.g. me, my, I) to the collective (e.g. our, we, us). Social identity is said to occur through three interrelated processes:

1 **Social categorisation** – whether you define yourself in collective rather than personal terms.
2 **Social identification** – whether you value the norms and behaviours of a group.
3 **Social comparison** – whether you can distinguish between the in-group and out-group.

In the case of online groups or communities, platforms such as Facebook groups, pages, and subreddits may permit people to connect to these communi-ties on both a psychological and social level, but their membership does not require them to interact directly or engage with other members. In this sense, relationships online can be complex and certainly more than just how many 'Facebook friends' you have. Despite the fact that these online groups and com-munities may not often readily be considered 'social', I would argue that they constitute important parts of human connection and group behaviour, all of which support relationships.

A final issue to note is whether all social media use is primarily 'social' at all. In the main, we use social media for socialising, connection, and relation-ships – all of which underpin the need for relatedness or belonging with others. However, there are a range of uses where the motivation is not to be social, but there are commercial or political reasons instead. This would fall under the category of organisational use of social media, which is a powerful marketing tool to cultivate consumer engagement, build relationships with customers, and advertise products and services (Dwivedi, Ismagilova, Hughes, Carlson, Filieri, Jacobson et al., 2020; Tiago & Verissimo, 2014). Whilst some of the afore-mentioned behaviours may be relevant here to understand different levels of 'active' use, there are conceptual issues regarding whether organisational use should be situated within the same models, or they are better understood as something other than 'socialness' (Kaye, 2021). Relationship formation and maintenance are still relevant issues here but clearly represent different types of relationships to our personal or even professional ones.

Conclusion

When exploring relationships on social media, we have to remember that they are not exclusive to social media. Social media is one of many contexts which can help connect people across networks, support relationship maintenance, and develop a range of social opportunities. These opportunities for being social are not always interactive or bidirectional but may simply occur by being in the same social space with similar others, which can provide a sense of human connected-ness and belonging. We also have to be mindful that social media is diverse, and whilst we tend to focus on personal relationships that may be driven socially, there are commercial and political uses which do not fit neatly into the current theoretical frameworks for understanding the 'socialness' of social media.

Box 7.2: Thinking activity

- Do you have any online-exclusive friends/contacts?
- What are the behaviours you use to maintain these friendships?
- Do your behaviours take place across platforms? If so, what purpose does this serve for friendship maintenance?

Box 7.3: Take-home message

Relationships online can be rather diverse and often can bring challenges when multiple types of relationships co-exist in a given online space. There is also the issue about how relationship formation and maintenance can function across contexts (online and real-world, as well as across multiple online platforms), and how this may impact upon things like relationship quality and impression management. Whilst online-exclusive relationships do exist, in most cases it is incorrect to describe relationships or friends based on whether they are 'online' of 'offline', as often there can be a high degree of overlap.

References

Anderson, M., Vogels, E.A., & Turner, E. (2020). *The virtues and downsides of online dating*. Washington, DC: Pew Research Center. Retrieved 3 February 2021 from: https://www.pewresearch.org/internet/2020/02/06/the-virtues-and-downsides-of-online-dating/

Bargh, J.A., McKenna, K.Y.A., & Fitzsimons, G.M. (2002). Can you see the real me? Activation and expression of the 'true self' on the Internet. *Journal of Social Issues, 58* (1), 33–48. https://doi.org/10.1111/1540-4560.00247

Briggle, A. (2008). Real friends: How the Internet can foster friendship. *Ethics and Information Technology, 10*, 71–79. https://doi.org/10.1007/s10676-008-9160-z

Buss, D.M. (1985). Human mate selection. *American Scientist, 73* (1), 47–51.

Cocking, S., & Matthews, S. (2000). Unreal friends. *Ethics and Information Technology, 2*, 223–231. https://doi.org/10.1023/A:1011414704851

Cummings, J.N., Sproull, L., & Kiesler, S.B. (2002). Beyond hearing: Where the real-world and online support meet. *Group Dynamics: Theory, Research, and Practice, 6* (1), 78–88. https://doi.org/10.1037/1089-2699.6.1.78

Darbyshire, D.E., Kirk, C., Wall, H.J., & Kaye, L.K. (2016). Don't judge a (Face)book by its cover: Exploring judgement accuracy of others' personality on Facebook. *Computers in Human Behavior, 58*, 380–387. https://doi.org/10.1016/j.chb.2016.01.021

Davidson, B.I., & Joinson, A.N. (2021). Shape shifting across social media. *Social Media and Society, 7* (1), 1–11. https://doi.org/10.1177/2056305121990632

Davis, J.L., & Jurgenson, N. (2014). Context collapse: Theorizing context collusions and collisions. *Information, Communication & Society, 17* (4), 476–485. https://doi.org/10.1080/1369118X.2014.888458

De Silva, M.J., McKenzie, K., Harpham, T., & Huttly, S.R. (2005). Social capital and mental illness: A systematic review. *Journal of Epidemiology and Community Health, 59* (8), 619–627. https://doi.org/10.1136/jech.2004.029678

Dunbar, R.I.M. (2010). *How many friends does one person need? Dunbar's number and other evolutionary quirks*. London: Faber & Faber.

Dunbar, R.I.M. (2016). Do online social media cut through the constraints that limit the size of offline social networks? *Royal Society Open Science, 3* (1), 150292. https://doi.org/10.1098/rsos.150292

Dwivedi, Y.K., Ismagilova, E., Hughes, D.L., Carlson, J., Filieri, R., Jacobson, J. et al. (2020). Setting the future of digital and social media marketing research: Perspectives and research propositions. *International Journal of Information Management, 59*, 102168. https://doi.org/10.1016/j.ijinfomgt.2020.102168

Ellison, N.B., Steinfield, C., & Lampe, C. (2007). The benefits of Facebook 'friends': Social capital and college students' use of online social network sites. *Journal of Computer-Mediated Communication, 12* (4), 1143–1168. https://doi.org/10.1111/j.1083-6101.2007.00367.x

Fox Hamilton, N., Fullwood, C., & Kirwan, G. (2015). Language in online dating texts: Trait identification, homophily, and their effect on attraction. In B.K. Wiederhold, G. Riva, & M.D. Wiederhold (Eds.), *Annual review of cybertherapy and telemedicine*, Vol. 13. (pp. 112–116). Amsterdam: IOS Press.

Fröding, M., & Peterson, M. (2012). Why virtual friendship is no genuine friendship. *Ethics and Information Technology, 14*, 201–207. https://doi.org/10.1007/s10676-011-9284-4

Helliwell, J.F., & Putnam, R.D. (2004). The social context of well-being. *Philosophical Transactions of the Royal Society B, 359* (1449), 1435–1446. https://doi.org/10.1098/rstb.2004.1522

Hoang, T.A., Lim, E.P., Achananuparp, P., Jiang, J., & Teow, L.N. (2011). Modeling socialness in dynamic social networks. In *Proceedings of the 2011 International Conference on Advances in Social Networks Analysis and Mining* (pp. 244–350). https://doi.org/10.1109/ASONAM.2011.91

Hogan, B. (2010). The presentation of self in the age of social media: Distinguishing performances and exhibitions online. *Bulletin of Science, Technology & Society, 30* (6), 377–386. https://doi.org/10.1177/0270467610385893

Jonason, P.K., & Antoon, C.N. (2019). Mate preferences for educated partners: Similarities and differences in the sexes depend on mating context. *Personality and Individual Differences, 148,* 57–61. https://doi.org/10.1016/j.paid.2019.05.036

Kaye, L.K. (2021). Exploring 'socialness' in social media. *Computers in Human Behavior Reports, 3,* 100083. https://doi.org/10.1016/j.chbr.2021.100083

Kaye, L.K., & Quinn, S. (2020). Psychosocial outcomes associated with engagement with online chat systems. *International Journal of Human-Computer Interaction, 36* (2), 190–198. https://doi.org/10.1080/10447318.2019.1620524

Marder, B., Joinson, A., Shankar, A., & Thirlaway, K. (2016). Strength matters: Self-presentation to the strongest audience rather than lowest common denominator when faced with multiple audiences in social network sites. *Computers in Human Behavior, 61,* 56–62. https://doi.org/10.1016/j.chb.2016.03.005

Marwick, A.E., & Boyd, D. (2011). I tweet honestly, I tweet passionately: Twitter users, context collapse, and the imagined audience. *New Media & Society, 13,* 114–133. https://doi.org/10.1177/1461444810365313

Meier, A., & Reinecke, L. (2020). Computer-mediated communication, social media and mental health: A conceptual and empirical meta-review. *Communication Research.* https://doi.org/10.1177/0093650220958224

Meske, C., Junglas, I., Schneider, J., & Jaakonmäki, R. (2019). How social is your social network? Toward a measurement model. In *Proceedings of the 40th International Conference on Information Systems (ICIS 2019)*, Munich, 15–18 December.

Nabi, R.L., Prestin, A., & So, J. (2013). Facebook friends with (health) benefits? Exploring social network site use and perceptions of social support, stress, and well-being. *Cyberpsychology, Behavior and Social Networking, 16* (10), 721–727. https://doi.org/10.1089/cyber.2012.0521

Neuman, S.B. (1988). The displacement effect: Assessing the relation between television viewing and reading performance. *Reading Research Quarterly, 23* (4), 414–440. https://doi.org/10.2307/747641

Pagani, M., Hofacker, C.F., & Goldsmith, R.E. (2011). The influence of personality on active and passive use of social networking sites. *Psychology & Marketing, 28* (5), 441–456. https://doi.org/10.1002/mar.20395

Putnam, R.D. (2000). *Bowling alone.* New York: Simon & Schuster.

Rafaeli, S. (1988). Interactivity: From new media to communication. In R.P. Hawkins, J.M. Wiemann, & S. Pingree (Eds.), *Advancing communication science: Merging mass and interpersonal process* (pp. 110–134). Newbury Park, CA: Sage.

Ryan, T., Allen, K.A., Gray, D.L., & McInerney, D.M. (2017). How social are social media? A review of online social behaviour and connectedness. *Journal of Relationships Research, 8,* e8. https://doi.org/10.1017/jrr.2017.13

Selim, H., Scott, G.G., & Kaye, L.K. (2021). A cross-cultural study to explore the differential impacts of online social capital on psychosocial outcomes. *Computers in Human Behavior Reports, 3,* 100087. https://doi.org/10.1016/j.chbr.2021.100087

Shaw, D., Pennington, C.R., Ngombe, N., Kessler, K., & Kaye, L.K. (2021). It's not what you do, it's the way that you do it: An experimental task delineates among styles of behaviour on social networking sites and psychosocial measures. *Author pre-print.* https://psyarxiv.com/ztkmv/

Shim, M., Lee, M., & Park, S. (2008). Photograph use on social network sites among South Korean college students: The role of public and private self-consciousness. *CyberPsychology & Behavior, 11* (4), 489–493. https://doi.org/10.1089/cpb.2007.0104

Snodgrass, J.G., Lacy, M.G., Dengah, H.J.F., & Fagan, J. (2011). Enhancing one life rather than living two: Playing MMOs with offline friends. *Computers in Human Behavior, 27* (3), 1211–1222. https://doi.org/10.1016/j.chb.2011.01.001

Stanton-Salazar, R.D., & Dornbusch, S.M. (1995). Social capital and the reproduction of inequality: Information networks among Mexican-origin high school students. *Sociology of. Education, 68* (2), 116–135. https://doi.org/10.2307/2112778

Sutcliffe, A.G., Binder, J.F., & Dunbar, R.I.M. (2018). Activity in social media and intimacy in social relationships. *Computers in Human Behavior, 85,* 227–235. https://doi.org/10.1016/j.chb.2018.03.050

Tajfel, H. (1978). *Differentiation between social groups.* London: Academic Press.

Tajfel, H. (1979). Individuals and groups in social psychology. *British Journal of Social and Clinical Psychology, 18* (2), 183–190. https://doi.org/10.1111/j.2044-8260.1979.tb00324.x

Tajfel, H., & Turner, J. (1979). An integrative theory of inter-group conflict. In J.A. Williams & S. Worchel (Eds.), *The social psychology of inter-group relations* (pp. 33–47). Belmont, CA: Wadsworth.

Tiago, M.T.P.M.B., & Verissimo, J.M.C. (2014). Digital marketing and social media: Why bother? *Business Horizons, 57* (6), 703–708. https://doi.org/10.1016/j.bushor.2014.07.002

Valkenburg, P.M., & Peter, J. (2009). Social consequences of the Internet for adolescents: A decade of research. *Current Directions in Psychological Science, 18* (1), 1–5. https://doi.org/10.1111/j.1467-8721.2009.01595.x

Valkenburg, P.M., van Driel, I.I., & Beyens, I. (2021). The associations of active and passive media use with well-being: A critical scoping review. *Author pre-print.* https://doi.org/10.31234/osf.io/j6xqz

Vitak, J. (2012). The impact of context collapse and privacy on social network site disclosures. *Journal of Broadcasting & Electronic Media, 56* (4), 451–70. https://doi.org/10.1080/08838151.2012.732140

Wall, H.J., Kaye, L.K., & Malone, S.A. (2016). An exploration of psychological factors on emoticon usage and implications for judgement accuracy. *Computers in Human Behavior, 62,* 70–78. https://doi.org/10.1016/j.chb.2016.03.040

Wang, J.L., Gaskin, J., Rost, D.H., & Gentile, D.A. (2018). The reciprocal relationship between passive social networking site (SNS) usage and users' subjective well-being. *Social Science Computer Review, 36* (5), 511–522. https://doi.org/10.1177/0894439317721981

Yu, R.P. (2016). The relationship between passive and active non-political social media use and political expression on Facebook and Twitter. *Computers in Human Behavior, 58,* 413–420. https://doi.org/10.1016/j.chb.2016.01.019

8 Social media and well-being

Box 8.1: Current questions

- How does using social media relate to mental health?
- Is social media making us obsessed with our appearance?

Following on from Chapter 7 on social media and relationships, this chapter addresses the issue of social media and well-being. One current prominent public debate is the extent to which social media impacts harmfully upon well-being. This debate often centres on how social media may displace meaningful social interactions and/or foster superficial connections that may be harmful to well-being, or may expose people to content that may be deemed harmful. This debate is not only central to public and societal debate, but is also a controversial issue in academic circles. In particular, much of the concern relates to young people's use of social media and how this may be feeding into the observed mental health crisis among this population.

Concerns about social media and mental health have been raised by recent research. However, the findings remain mixed, with little consensus between researchers. Many studies lack sufficient theoretical justification for why social media use should be related to well-being (Erfani & Adedin, 2018). Whilst there is some evidence for a negative correlation between social media use and young people's well-being (Twenge, 2019; Twenge & Campbell, 2019), other evidence suggests that these observed relationships are weak and there is little convincing longitudinal evidence about the causal impact of social media on well-being outcomes (Orben, Dienlin, & Przybylski, 2019; Odgers & Jensen, 2020; Orben, 2020; Orben & Przybylski, 2019).

Unfortunately, a lot of the social media and well-being debate gets conflated with 'screen-time' debates more generally (as discussed in Chapter 6). Certainly, it is the case that theoretical frameworks for understanding the impact of social media on well-being often conceptualise social media in rather general terms, or conflate it with 'digital media' or 'digital technology'. On any given social media platform, the range of types of content and behaviours that may occur is vast and largely personalised to the individual user. Therefore, it makes it rather difficult to clarify the conditions under which social media is likely to be beneficial to well-being or, conversely, detrimental. However, there may be a way to approach this issue. This brings us back to three core questions

I outlined in Chapter 2: what, how, and why? I will discuss these in turn in the following sections.

What?

When asking this question, I mean what content people are being exposed to when using social media. In Chapter 2, I raised the example of two people using the same social media platform for the same amount of time, but seeing different content, thus leading to two entirely different outcomes. As discussed in Chapter 7, social media is very diverse and there are many different types of content people are exposed to and consume via these platforms. We must acknowledge the fact that social media is not the equivalent of other forms of digital media (e.g. TV) and users are not simply passive consumers of content. Users are active in the way they engage with different types of content or interact on social media. Furthermore, the interactive nature of these platforms entails users experiencing transactions with other users that may be harmful or hurtful, suggesting that linear content consumption is not the only consideration when addressing the question of 'what'.

The literature has tended to focus on two main themes when speculating how the 'whats' of social media relate to well-being. These broadly consist of: (1) image-based social media, and (2) online harm (e.g. inappropriate content, cyberbullying, trolling, radicalisation). I will discuss each of these in turn.

Image-based social media

Image-based social media includes platforms such as Instagram and TikTok where users post profile updates via the medium of photos or videos (which can also include accompanying text). Of course, other social media platforms also permit multimedia sharing, but this is not the sole format of interactions and sharing content. Image-based platforms have been a concern from a well-being perspective, with claims that photos on these may promote unrealistic ideals particularly around body image (Fardouly & Vartanian, 2015). This is believed to occur through a process of social comparison where users compare themselves to the 'ideal' images they see on these platforms, which then has a detrimental impact on body satisfaction and self-esteem (Chua & Chang, 2016; Mackson, Brochu, & Schneider, 2019; Ryding & Kuss, 2020). Concerns have also been raised about how these social comparisons may trigger depressive episodes, particularly among those who already experience depression (Jiang & Ngien, 2020). In contrast, there is some evidence to suggest that young adults can use image-based platforms such as Instagram in positive ways through enhanced self-presentational capacity, which can support friendship development (Lee & Borah, 2020), and how aspects of social comparison can function for social adjustment and inspiration (Meier & Schäfer, 2018; Yang & Robinson, 2018). Furthermore, it has also been suggested that upward comparisons on social media can contribute to positive well-being (Meier, Gilbert, Börner, & Possler, 2020).

Essentially, to understand the extent to which image-based social media relates to well-being, it is important to know what type of multimedia is being posted and/or accessed. Although most of the existing literature in this area tends to focus on face or body photos, there is a wide range of types of photo content that users engage with (e.g. pets, foods, landscapes). In these cases, the theoretical insights from social comparison theory (Festinger, 1954), which tends to underpin work in this area, might not be pertinent to explain the associated psychosocial experiences. This calls for a greater level of attention in research when exploring the range of multimedia content users post, using techniques such as codebooks to categorise photo content (see Eftekhar Khansari, 2018) or content analyses of social media platforms (see Talbot, Gavin, Van Steen, & Morey, 2017). This would help ascertain how different combinations/amounts of image-based content impact on well-being, particularly in relation to body image and self-esteem.

Online harms

In addition to image-based content, there is also the concern of online harm as a result of the types of content and engagement people experience on social media. Such content may be triggering, distressing, radicalising, illegal, traumatic, or abusive. In the case of triggering, for example, this may involve content relating to pro-anorexia, self-harm, or suicide, which some people might be especially susceptible to. Minors are at particular risk of two specific types of online harms: health-related harms and sex-related harms (Slavtcheva-Petkova, Nash, & Bulger, 2015). Research in this area has found that exposure to self-harm on social media can predict users' self-harm behaviours and suicidality-related outcomes over time (Arendt, Scheer, & Romer, 2019). Other research suggests that exposure to content on social media which depicts risky behaviour may encourage users to adopt risky behaviours in the 'real world' (Branley & Covey, 2017). In the wider context, although recent reviews have suggested that online risks and existing 'real-world' risks are often interrelated (Livingstone & Smith, 2014), there are a range of emotional and psychosocial impacts from quite specific online harms, including post-traumatic stress disorder in cases of sexual solicitation (McHugh, Wisniewski, Rosson, & Carroll, 2018).

Although the range of online harms is extensive, there is a paucity of research on how exposure to harms such as illegal, distressing, traumatic, or inappropriate content relates more generally to user well-being, especially minors and young people. This is particularly surprising given the worrying nature of this issue and the fact that online harm is becoming increasingly situated in policy and proposed regulation frameworks (e.g. the UK Government's Online Harms White Paper, the Irish Government's Online Safety and Media Regulation Bill). However, one area that does have a fairly strong research-base is that of cyber-abuse, including cyberbullying and trolling, because cyber-abuse via social media is almost always detrimental to well-being. Though of course cyber-abuse and indeed other forms of abuse can occur in many different contexts, both online and in the 'real world'. But let's start with cyberbullying.

Cyberbullying is defined as 'an aggressive, intentional act carried out by a group or individual using electronic forms of contact, repeatedly and over time against a victim who cannot easily defend him or herself' (Smith, Mahdavi, Carvalho, Fisher, Russell, & Tippett, 2008: 376). Research on cyberbullying has tended to explore its nature (relative to more traditional forms of bullying) (Waasdorp & Bradshaw, 2015), factors relating to perpetration and victimisation (Calvete, Orue, Estévez, Villardón, & Padilla, 2010; Tokunaga, 2010), young people's perceptions (Vandebosch & Van Cleemput, 2008), teachers' and parents' perceptions (Macaulay, Betts, Stiller, & Kellezi, 2018), its impacts (Kowalski & Limber, 2013), and interventions (Popovac & Fine, 2018).

Being a victim of cyberbullying can be highly distressing. Indeed, it is clear that cyberbullying victimisation is related to a range of negative impacts on well-being, including emotional and behavioural problems in adolescence (Kim, Colwell, Kata, Boyle, & Georgiades, 2018), depression, and social anxiety (Fahy, Stansfield, Smuk, Smith, Cummins, & Clark, 2016).

Trolling is often discussed alongside cyberbullying, though it is distinctly different and unique to online settings. This is when someone makes unsolicited contact online, often in the form of comments about another person, often to prompt an emotional reaction. In more serious cases, it can amount to a form of harassment under anti-harassment laws. Although research has been conducted on the reasons for trolling, such as the profiles and risk factors associated with perpetration (e.g. Lopes & Yu, 2017; March, 2019; Navarro-Carrillo, Torres-Marín, & Carretero-Dios, 2021), little is known about the impact it has on its targets. This may be because there is often no specific 'victim', since trolling tends to be directed more at social media content or posts rather than an actual individual. However, when individuals do consider themselves victimised by trolling, some of the impacts may be similar to those of cyberbullying. However, in the absence of empirical findings, this is only speculative.

How?

The second question relates to how people use social media. Irrespective of content, the various ways in which people use social media will likely have a differential impact on their well-being (this relates to social media interactions, as discussed in Chapter 7). One specific area of interest is how 'active' or 'passive' people are on social media, which largely relates to the extent to which people are actually curating or interacting with the content of others online (Pagani, Hofacker, & Goldsmith, 2011; Shim, Lee, & Park, 2008). A so-called 'passive' user may be more likely to browse or observe others' content rather than curate their own (Pagani et al., 2011; Yu, 2016). In relation to well-being, it has been shown that passive use of social media is related to decreased well-being (Wang, Gaskin, Rost, & Gentile, 2018). In contrast, it has been shown that directed forms of social interaction (i.e. being more active) on social media can impact positively on well-being (Burke, Marlow, & Lento, 2010); that is, directed communication between users is related to enhanced bonding capital and decreased loneliness, whereas intensity of content consumption (i.e. more passive use) shows the converse trend (Burke et al., 2010). Along similar lines, Yang (2016) found that interacting and browsing on Instagram were related to reduced loneliness, whereas broadcasting was associated with higher loneliness. Therefore, the literature appears to suggest that the intensity of different types of social media behaviours (e.g. broadcasting, browsing, interacting, etc.) is key to a fuller understanding of the impacts of use on well-being. Recently, there has been a call to refine our understanding of these issues, and to devise a tool for measuring so-called 'passive' and 'active' use across the various social media platforms (Trifiro & Gerson, 2019). In 2013, Ellison and Boyd recommended 'activity-centric' approaches are needed to more fully understand the range of intricate behaviours involved in different types of 'active' use.

Moving on from how people use social media, there is the issue of use and overuse, which I outlined in detail in Chapter 3. Clearly, if a person is overusing social media, this may be detrimental to their well-being (Duradoni, Innocenti, & Guazzini, 2020). This is often discussed in terms of behavioural addiction, such as 'social media addiction', 'Facebook addiction', or 'social networking addiction' (Kuss & Griffiths, 2011, 2017). However, the converse may also be true for those who use social media sparingly, in the sense that they may be missing out on many social engagements. Recent theoretical perspectives lend themselves to this debate. For example, the Digital Goldilocks hypothesis (Przybylski & Weinstein, 2017) suggests that just the right amount of social media use may be most beneficial to well-being, whereas too much or not enough may have a detrimental impact. So, there appears to be an inverted-U shaped curve when correlating social media use with psychological well-being. This hypothesis has been extended to digital screen use more generally to explore how it impacts psychosocial functioning (Przybylski, Orben, & Weinstein, 2020).

Clearly, exploring quantities and intensities of use remains pertinent when theorising on the link between social media use and well-being, although we should be cautious about focusing entirely on volume of use. This should also be considered in the context of our final question, that of 'why'.

Why?

The final question relates to why people use social media, since irrespective of content or actual usage, people use social media for different reasons. For example, for some people it may be the only way of fulfilling social needs, while for others it may be a helpful supplement. And for others, there may be no social motivation at all!

The 'why' question can be approached in a number of ways. One way is to adopt the 'uses and gratifications' perspective that was alluded to in Chapter 3. This can be used to explore how people use social media for needs fulfilment. For example, this approach has been used to study how gratification-driven behaviours such as information-seeking and socialising may relate to behaviours such as online news-sharing (Lee & Ma, 2012). In this way, we can distinguish between social media use that is goal-driven or purposeful vs. that which is more generic in nature. This may be a key distinction when studying how social media use relates to well-being, such as how it can fulfil social needs or help people gain social support. Indeed, a prominent theme in social media and well-being from this perspective is that of how perceived social support from social media may mediate this relationship.

Utz and Breuer (2017) found that when comparing users and non-users of social media, users tended to report higher perceptions of online social support, although this was not related to perceptions of life satisfaction or reductions in stress over time. Other research has shown that active use of social media is positively related to online social support, which, in turn, is negatively related to depressed mood, specifically in girls (Frison & Eggermont, 2016). The nature of these findings likely corresponds to whether using social media for social support is goal-driven or simply an unintended experience of generic social media use. When theorising on social support, available frameworks suggest four key types of social support: emotional (compassion), tangible (good, services), informational, and companionship (social belonging, connection) (Langford, Bowsher, Maloney, & Lillis, 1997).

Some users may be more strategic or goal-driven in seeking specific types of social media (e.g. Facebook groups, community pages, etc.), as a way of seeking support for particular concerns such as health issues. It is important to understand how these more directed social media engagements impact on well-being, since there is much evidence to suggest that users engage in specific communities online for support relating to health concerns (Coulson, 2005; Coulson, Buchanan, & Aubeeluck, 2007; Wright, 2002). For example, people with physical and intellectual disabilities have been found to use online communities to garner social support for aspects of psychological well-being (Chadwick & Fullwood, 2018; Lee & Cho, 2019). In this way, these social media engagements may be somewhat purposeful and directed towards seeking varying forms of social support. However, thinking more generally, it is also the case that people may have a perception of social support simply from being in a social network, being connected to friends, and as a result of their more general social media use. This may be an unintended consequence of social media use yet still may relate favourably (or not) to well-being. For example, research has found that perceived social support corresponds to the perceived benefits of using social media for adolescents (Best, Manktelow, & Taylor, 2014). Additionally, other work shows that using social media such as Facebook predicts perceptions of social support, although does not necessarily have any subsequent impact on life satisfaction (Kim, 2014). Overall, then, it seems that to more fully understand the link between social media and well-being, it is important to know whether this behaviour is goal-directed or is more generic in nature. In addition, we need to account for the range of factors such as social support which may mediate this link. The variations across the literature in the way social media use and mediating factors have been operationalised may account for the mix of findings reported.

A final consideration in relation to the question of 'why' is that of professional use of social media. That is, someone's reason for using social media may be simply because it is their job to manage an organisational social media account. Despite digital marketing and social media manager roles being a prominent part of twenty-first-century organisational culture, we lack research on whether the impacts of social media on well-being are different for personal and professional use (Kaye, 2021). The only evidence available has focused more on employee use of social media and how this tends to relate to things like productivity, team relations, and other work-related outcomes (Ewing, Men, & O'Neil, 2019; Robertson & Kee, 2017; Yu, Cao, Lui, & Wang, 2018). Cyberpsychology research needs to address how organisational use of social media impacts well-being, owing to the pressures social media managers are under to uphold organisational reputation. In addition, they may intercept a substantial amount of abusive messaging which may be traumatic for them. Finally, social media managers may find it difficult to distinguish between their private and working lives when using the same social media platforms for their personal use as they do at work.

Conclusion

This chapter has interrogated how social media may relate to well-being through three lenses: what, how, and why. Clearly, the link between social media and well-being is not always clear, causal, and linear. The complexities of the issue relate to the interaction of all of the three lenses previously outlined, but also a range of individual-level factors about users themselves which help to determine the way in which social media is used and its function in daily life. Figure 8.1 illustrates the main thrust of this chapter, whose focus was on social media use and well-being.

Figure 8.1. Summary of how the lenses of social media behaviours may relate to well-being

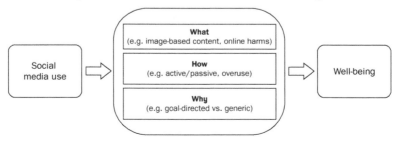

Box 8.2: Thinking activity

To better understand the extent to which the 'what', the 'how', and the 'why' of social media relate to well-being, consider the following questions:

- How can researchers best quantify/measure people's exposure/engagement with certain types of online content on social media?
- How could people's levels of engagement or interactions with social media content be measured more successfully?
- What are the reasons that people use social media for? Are these different across platforms?

Box 8.3: Take-home message

The well-being effects of social media are complex. To understand these more fully, we need to move away from talking about social media use *per se*, and instead look at these effects through the lens of what, how, and why and how these each interact with one another.

References

Arendt, F., Scheer, S., & Romer, D. (2019). Effects of exposure to self-harm on social media: Evidence from a two-wave panel study among young adults. *New Media & Society, 21* (11/12), 2422–2442. https://doi.org/10.1177/1461444819850106

Best, P., Manktelow, R., & Taylor, B. (2014). Online communication, social media and adolescent wellbeing: A systematic narrative review. *Children and Youth Services Review, 41*, 27–36. https://doi.org/10.1016/j.childyouth.2014.03.001

Branley, D.B., & Covey, J. (2017). Is exposure to online content depicting risky behavior related to viewers' own risky behavior offline? *Computers in Human Behavior, 75*, 283–287. https://doi.org/10.1016/j.chb.2017.05.023

Burke, M., Marlow, C., & Lento, T. (2010). Social network activity and social well-being. In *Proceedings of the SIGCHI Conference on Human Factors in Computing Systems* (pp. 1909–1912), April 2020. https://doi.org/10.1145/1753326.1753613

Calvete, E., Orue, I., Estévez, A., Villardón, L., & Padilla, P. (2010). Cyberbullying in adolescents: Modalities and aggressors' profile. *Computers in Human Behavior, 26* (5), 1128–1135. https://doi.org/10.1016/j.chb.2010.03.017

Chadwick, D.D., & Fullwood, C. (2018). An online life like any other: Identity, self-determination and social networking among adults with intellectual disabilities. *Cyberpsychology, Behavior & Social Networking, 21* (1), 56–64. https://doi.org/10.1089/cyber.2016.0689

Chua, T.H.H., & Chang, L. (2016). Follow me and like my beautiful selfies: Singapore teenage girls' engagement in self-presentation and peer comparison on social media. *Computers in Human Behavior, 55* (Part A), 190–197. https://doi.org/10.1016/j.chb.2015.09.011

Coulson, N.S. (2005). Receiving social support online: An analysis of a computer-mediated support group for individuals living with irritable bowel syndrome. *Cyberpsychology and Behavior, 8* (6), 580–584. https://doi.org/10.1089/cpb.2005.8.580

Coulson, N.S., Buchanan, H., & Aubeeluck, A. (2007). Social support in cyberspace: A content analysis of communication within a Huntington's disease online support group. *Patient Education and Counseling, 68* (2), 173–178. https://doi.org/10.1016/j.pec.2007.06.002

Duradoni, M., Innocenti, F., & Guazzini, A. (2020). Well-being and social media: A systematic review of Bergen addiction scales. *Future Internet, 12* (2), 24. https://doi.org/10.3390/fi12020024

Eftekhar Khansari, A. (2018). *Personality as a predictor of visual self-presentation and motivations for photo sharing via social media.* Unpublished doctoral thesis, University of Wolverhampton.

Ellison, N.B., & Boyd, D.M. (2013). Sociality through social network sites. In W.H. Dutton (Ed.), *The Oxford handbook of internet studies* (pp. 151–172). Oxford: Oxford University Press.

Erfani, S.S., & Adedin, B. (2018). Impacts of the use of social network sites on users' psychological well-being: A systematic review. *Journal of the Association for Information Science and Technology, 69* (7), 900–912. https://doi.org/10.1002/asi.24015

Ewing, M., Men, L.R., & O'Neil, J. (2019). Using social media to engage employees: Insights from internal communication managers. *International Journal of Strategic Communication, 13* (2), 110–132. https://doi.org/10.1080/1553118X.2019.1575830

Fahy, A.E., Stansfield, S.A., Smuk, M., Smith, S.R., Cummins, S., & Clark, C. (2016). Longitudinal associations between cyberbullying involvement and adolescent mental health. *Journal of Adolescent Health, 59* (5), 502–509. https://doi.org/10.1016/j.jadohealth.2016.06.006

Fardouly, J., & Vartanian, L.R. (2015). Negative comparisons about one's appearance mediate the relationship between Facebook usage and body image concerns. *Body Image, 12,* 82–88. https://doi.org/10.1016/J.BODYIM.2014.10.004

Festinger L. (1954). A theory of social comparison processes. *Human Relations, 7* (2), 117–140. https://doi.org/10.1177/001872675400700202

Frison, E., & Eggermont, S. (2016). Exploring the relationships between different types of Facebook use, perceived online social support, and adolescents' depressed mood. *Social Science Computer Review, 34* (2), 153–171. https://doi.org/10.1177/0894439314567449

Jiang, S., & Ngien, A. (2020). The effects of Instagram use, social comparison, and self-esteem on social anxiety: A survey study in Singapore. *Social Media and Society, 6* (2). https://doi.org/10.1177/2056305120912488

Kaye, L.K. (2021). Exploring 'socialness' in social media. *Computers in Human Behavior Reports, 3,* 100083. https://doi.org/10.1016/j.chbr.2021.100083

Kim, H. (2014). Enacted social support on social media and subjective well-being. *International Journal of Communication, 8,* 2340–2342. https://ijoc.org/index.php/ijoc/article/view/2243

Kim, S., Colwell, S.R., Kata, A., Boyle, M.H., & Georgiades, K. (2018). Cyberbullying victimization and adolescent mental health: Evidence of differential effects by sex and mental health problem type. *Journal of Youth and Adolescence, 47,* 661–672. https://doi.org/10.1007/s10964-017-0678-4

Kowalski, R.M., & Limber, S.P. (2013). Psychological, physical, and academic correlates of cyberbullying and traditional bullying. *Journal of Adolescent Health, 53* (1), S13–S20. https://doi.org/10.1016/j.jadohealth.2012.09.018

Kuss, D.J., & Griffiths, M.D. (2011). Online social networking and addiction – a review of the psychological literature. *International Journal of Environmental Research and Public Health, 8* (12), 3528–3552. https://doi.org/10.3390/ijerph8093528

Kuss, D.J., & Griffiths, M.D. (2017). Social networking sites and addiction: ten lessons learned. *International Journal of Environmental Research and Public Health, 14* (3), 311. https://doi.org/10.3390/ijerph14030311

Langford, C.P., Bowsher, J., Maloney, J.P., & Lillis, P.P. (1997). Social support: A conceptual analysis. *Journal of Advanced Nursing, 25* (1), 95–100. https://doi.org/10.1046/j.1365-2648.1997.1997025095.x

Lee, C.S., & Ma, L. (2012). News sharing in social media: The effect of gratifications and prior experience. *Computers in Human Behavior, 28* (2), 331–339. https://doi.org/10.1016/j.chb.2011.10.002

Lee, D.K.L., & Borah, P. (2020). Self-presentation on Instagram and friendship development among young adults: A moderated mediation model of media richness, perceived functionality, and openness. *Computers in Human Behavior, 103*, 57–66. https://doi.org/10.1016/j.chb.2019.09.017

Lee, H.E., & Cho, J. (2019). Social media use and well-being in people with physical disabilities: Influence of SNS and online community uses on social support, depression, and psychological disposition. *Health Communication, 34* (9), 1043–1052. https://doi.org/10.1080/10410236.2018.1455138

Livingstone, S., & Smith, P.K. (2014). Annual research review: Harms experienced by child users of online and mobile technologies: The nature, prevalence and management of sexual and aggressive risks in the digital age. *Journal of Child Psychology and Psychiatry, 55* (6), 635–654. https://doi.org/10.1111/jcpp.12197

Lopes, B., & Yu, H. (2017). Who do you troll and why: An investigation into the relationship between the Dark Triad Personalities and online trolling behaviours towards popular and less popular Facebook profiles. *Computers in Human Behavior, 77*, 69–76. https://doi.org/10.1016/j.chb.2017.08.036

Macaulay, P.J.R., Betts, L.R., Stiller, J., & Kellezi, B. (2018). Perceptions and responses towards cyberbullying: A systematic review of teachers in the education system. *Aggression and Violent Behavior, 43*, 1–12. https://doi.org/10.1016/j.avb.2018.08.004

Mackson, S.B., Brochu, P.M., & Schneider, B.A. (2019). Instagram: Friend or foe? The application's association with psychological well-being. *New Media &d Society, 21* (10), 2160–2182. https://doi.org/10.1177/1461444819840021

March, E. (2019). Psychopathy, sadism, empathy, and the motivation to cause harm: New evidence confirms malevolent nature of the Internet troll. *Personality and Individual Differences, 141*, 133–137. https://doi.org/10.1016/j.paid.2019.01.001

McHugh, B.C., Wisniewski, P., Rosson, M.B., & Carroll, J.M. (2018). When social media traumatizes teens: The roles of online risk exposure, coping, and post-traumatic stress. *Internet Research, 28* (5), 1169–1188, https://doi.org/10.1108/IntR-02-2017-0077

Meier, A., Gilbert, A., Börner, S., & Possler, D. (2020). Instagram inspiration: How upward comparison on social network sites can contribute to well-being. *Journal of Communication, 70* (5), 721–743. https://doi.org/10.1093/joc/jqaa025

Meier, A., & Schäfer, S. (2018). The positive side of social comparison on social network sites: How envy can drive inspiration on Instagram. *Cyberpsychology, Behavior, and Social Networking, 21* (7), 411—417. http://doi.org/10.1089/cyber.2017.0708

Navarro-Carrillo, G., Torres-Marín, J., & Carretero-Dios, H. (2021). Do trolls just want to have fun? Assessing the role of humor-related traits in online trolling behavior. *Computers in Human Behavior, 114*, 106551. https://doi.org/10.1016/j.chb.2020.106551

Odgers, C.L., & Jensen, M.R. (2020). Annual research review: Adolescent mental health in the digital age: Facts, fears, and future directions. *Journal of Child Psychology and Psychiatry, 61* (3), 336–348. https://doi.org/10.1111/jcpp.13190

Orben, A. (2020). Teenagers, screens and social media: A narrative review of reviews and key studies. *Social Psychiatry and Psychiatric Epidemiology, 55,* 407–414. https://doi.org/10.1007/s00127-019-01825-4

Orben, A., Dienlin, T., & Przybylski, A.K. (2019). Social media's enduring effect on adolescent life satisfaction. *Proceedings of the National Academy of Sciences USA, 116* (21), 10226–10228. https://doi.org/10.1073/pnas.1902058116

Orben, A., & Przybylski, A.K. (2019). The association between adolescent well-being and digital technology use. *Nature Human Behaviour, 3,* 173–182. https://doi.org/10.1038/s41562-018-0506-1

Pagani, M., Hofacker, C.F., & Goldsmith, R.E. (2011). The influence of personality on active and passive use of social networking sites. *Psychology & Marketing, 28* (5), 441–456. https://doi.org/10.1002/mar.20395

Popovac, M., & Fine, P. (2018). An intervention using the Information-Motivation-Behavioural Skills Model: Tackling cyberaggression and cyberbullying in South African adolescents. In M. Campbell & S. Bauman (Eds.), *Reducing cyberbullying in schools: International evidence-based best practices* (pp. 225–244). London: Academic Press.

Przybylski, A.K., Orben, A., & Weinstein, N. (2020). How much is too much? Examining the relationship between digital screen engagement and psychosocial functioning in a confirmatory cohort study. *Journal of the American Academy of Child & Adolescent Psychiatry, 59* (9), 1080–1088. https://doi.org/10.1016/j.jaac.2019.06.017

Przybylski, A.K., & Weinstein, N. (2017). A large-scale test of the Goldilocks hypothesis: Quantifying the relations between digital-screen use and the mental well-being of adolescents. *Psychological Science, 28* (2), 204–215. https://doi.org/10.1177/0956797616678438

Robertson, B.W., & Kee, K.F. (2017). Social media at work: The roles of job satisfaction, employment status, and Facebook use with co-workers. *Computers in Human Behavior, 70,* 191–196. https://doi.org/10.1016/j.chb.2016.12.080

Ryding, F.C., & Kuss, D.J. (2020). The use of social networking sites, body image dissatisfaction, and body dysmorphic disorder: A systematic review of psychological research. *Psychology of Popular Media, 9* (4), 412–435. https://doi.org/10.1037/ppm0000264

Shim, M., Lee, M., & Park, S. (2008). Photograph use on social network sites among South Korean college students: The role of public and private self-consciousness. *CyberPsychology & Behavior, 11* (4), 489–493. https://doi.org/10.1089/cpb.2007.0104

Slavtcheva-Petkova, V., Nash, V.J., & Bulger, M. (2015). Evidence on the extent of harms experienced by children as a result of online risks: Implications for policy and research. *Information, Communication and Society, 19* (1), 48–62. https://doi.org/10.1080/1369118X.2014.934387

Smith, P.K., Mahdavi, J., Carvalho, M., Fisher, S., Russell, S., & Tippett, N. (2008). Cyberbullying: Its nature and impact in secondary school pupils. *Journal of Child Psychology and Psychiatry, 49* (4), 376–385. https://doi.org/10.1111/j.1469-7610.2007.01846.x

Talbot, C.V., Gavin, J., Van Steen, T., & Morey, Y. (2017). A content analysis of thinspiration, fitspiration, and bonespiration imagery on social media. *Journal of Eating Disorders, 5,* 40. https://doi.org/10.1186/s40337-017-0170-2

Tokunaga, R.S. (2010). Following you home from school: A critical review and synthesis of research on cyberbullying victimization. *Computers in Human Behavior, 26* (3), 277–287. https://doi.org/10.1016/j.chb.2009.11.014

Trifiro, B.M., & Gerson, J. (2019). Social media usage patterns: Research note regarding the lack of universal validated measures for active and passive use. *Social Media and Society, 5* (2). https://doi.org/10.1177/2056305119848743

Twenge, J.M. (2019). More time on technology, less happiness? Associations between digital-media use and psychological well-being. *Current Directions in Psychological Science, 28* (4), 372–379. https://doi.org/10.1177/0963721419838244

Twenge, J.M., & Campbell, W.K. (2019). Media use is linked to lower psychological well-being: Evidence from three datasets. *Psychiatric Quarterly, 90* (2), 311–331. https://doi.org/10.1007/s11126-019-09630-7

Utz, S., & Breuer, J. (2017). The relationship between use of social network sites, online social support, and well-being: Results from a six-wave longitudinal study. *Journal of Media Psychology: Theories, Methods, and Applications, 29* (3), 115–125. http://dx.doi.org/10.1027/1864-1105/a000222

Vandebosch, H., & Van Cleemput, K. (2008). Defining cyberbullying: A qualitative research into the perceptions of youngsters. *CyberPsychology & Behavior, 11* (4), 499–503. http://doi.org/10.1089/cpb.2007.0042

Waasdorp, T.E., & Bradshaw, C.P. (2015). The overlap between cyberbullying and traditional bullying. *Journal of Adolescent Health, 56* (5), 483–488. https://doi.org/10.1016/j.jadohealth.2014.12.002

Wang, J.L., Gaskin, J., Rost, D.H., & Gentile, D.A. (2018). The reciprocal relationship between passive social networking site (SNS) usage and users' subjective well-being. *Social Science Computer Review, 36* (5), 511–522. https://doi.org/10.1177/0894439317721981

Wright, K. (2002). Social support within an on-line cancer community: An assessment of emotional support, perceptions of advantages and disadvantages, and motives for using the community from a communication perspective. *Journal of Applied Communication Research, 30* (3), 195–209. https://doi.org/10.1080/00909880216586

Yang, C.C. (2016). Instagram use, loneliness, and social comparison orientation: Interact and browse on social media, but don't compare. *Cyberpsychology, Behavior, and Social Networking, 19* (12), 703–708. https://doi.org/10.1089/cyber.2016.0201

Yang, C.C. & Robinson, A. (2018). Not necessarily detrimental: Two social comparison orientations and their associations with social media use and college social adjustment. *Computers in Human Behavior, 84*, 49–57. https://doi.org/10.1016/j.chb.2018.02.020

Yu, L., Cao, X., Lui, Z., & Wang, J. (2018). Excessive social media use at work: Exploring the effects of social media overload on job performance. *Information Technology & People, 31* (6), 1091–1112. https://doi.org/10.1108/ITP-10-2016-0237

Yu, R.P. (2016). The relationship between passive and active non-political social media use and political expression on Facebook and Twitter. *Computers in Human Behavior, 58*, 413–420. https://doi.org/10.1016/j.chb.2016.01.019

9 Digital games effects

> **Box 9.1: Current questions**
>
> - Does playing violent video games relate to real-world aggression?
> - How much is too much gaming?
> - Can digital games be used in education?

Existing literature shows how digital gaming is related to a range of outcomes. These include psychosocial (e.g. well-being, loneliness), cognitive (aggressive cognition, visual attention), social (e.g. out-group bias, group cohesion), emotional (e.g. mood), and physiological (e.g. arousal), all of which may vary in the longevity of their effects (i.e. short- or long-term impacts). Although research on the psychology of digital gaming has explored a range of issues, including player demographics, motivations to play, and player experiences, the main focus in academic and public debates relates to the likely effects or outcomes of gaming. This has predominately focused on two key issues: the anti-social effects of (violent) game content, and the pathological impacts of excessive play. Although I use the terms 'effects' and 'impacts' here, it is important to recognise that much of the literature in this field is cross-sectional in nature, and therefore it is perhaps better instead to consider these as 'correlates'.

Debates in this field are typically focused on the question of whether digital games are good or bad for you. Unfortunately, there is no simple answer to this question. Notwithstanding the nuances which need to be acknowledged (discussed in this chapter), the sheer diversity of games and gaming means it is not appropriate to make categorical generalisations. Framing digital games as either good or bad is not helpful to progressing our understanding of these issues.

Perhaps a more helpful approach to explore digital gaming effects is to adopt a framework that acknowledges the various facets of games and gaming. This framework, which is shown in Figure 9.1, consists of the following five facets: what, how, why, where, and who. The remainder of this chapter will review the current evidence in line with this framework.

A further issue, which I raised briefly in Chapter 2, relates to expected (behavioural) effects. That is, I previously noted that a major limitation of the 'technology effects' literature in general, and relevant to the wide-ranging disparate literature on digital gaming effects in particular, is that there is generally a lack of robust theories underpinning behaviour change. Behaviour is vastly complex and motivated by a broad range of factors, which are evident

Figure 9.1. Summary of the range of facets that will determine the effects of digital games/gaming

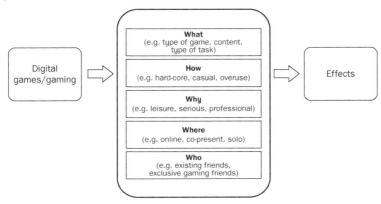

in theoretical models of behaviour change such as the 'COM-B system' (Michie, van Stralen, & West, 2011) and the Theory of Planned Behaviour (Ajzen, 1985, 1991; Ajzen & Madden, 1986). However, studies on digital gaming effects have often not integrated robust behaviour change models to help explain how exposure to or engagement with digital games or gaming would be expected to result in specific behavioural outcomes. For example, skill acquisition, one outcome of (action) gaming, is perhaps easier to explain via changes in attentional processes, whereas prosocial behaviour associated with engaging in games depicting refugees would require alternative theoretical models. Whilst some focal areas in this field are better integrated with theory than others, overall models specifically explaining *behavioural* outcomes of digital games are less robust and inconsistent. For a good review of video games and behaviour change, see McCain, Morrison, and Ahn (2019), who outline some of the main factors underpinning psychosocial pathways to behaviour, including motivation, reinforcement, personalisation, and embodiment.

What

A prominent debate in the field of digital gaming is that of how the content of games may have anti-social effects, including aggressive thoughts and behaviour. This is largely focused on how repeated exposure to any violent content in games may encourage access to aggressive scripts and thus promote aggressive responding, and/or reduced sensitivity to real-world violence (Anderson, Shibuya, Ihori, Swing, Bushman, Sakamoto et al., 2010; DeLisi, Vaughn, Gentile, Anderson, & Shook, 2013). This debate has populated this field for decades, with some researchers continuously showing evidence of aggressive effects (Anderson, Bushman, Bartholow, Cantor, Christakis, Coyne et al., 2017), others demonstrating minimal or null effects (Ferguson, 2015), and still others who question the integrity and quality of research in this area (Elson & Ferguson, 2014).

Although this is a controversial area of study, there are a number of things to note. First, not all games involve violent content and thus this debate does not apply to them. Second, there is an associated area of work that shows that when participants engage in a competitive game task, they are more likely to display short-term aggressive or less prosocial responding than when engaged in a cooperative task (discussed later in this chapter). Therefore, there is an issue here of how content may interact with the type of task players are engaged in, adding a further layer of complexity to the issue. Third, an exclusive focus on aggressive effects somewhat side-lines efforts to explore the range of effects of digital games, and takes a rather restrictive view of games and gaming. For example, some research has highlighted that both engagement with prosocial content and engaging cooperatively in gaming are associated with prosocial attitudes and behaviours following gameplay (Greitemeyer & Osswald, 2010; Stiff & Bowen, 2016; Stiff & Kedra, 2020). Furthermore, when looking at skill acquisition, it has been reported that engagement in fast-paced action games promotes visual attention skills (Green & Bavelier, 2003, 2006, 2007). Therefore, different types of games and content should be a key consideration before making broad claims about whether games are good or bad for you. Finally, such a focus on game content tends to preclude the fact that players engage as part of a process. That is, engaging with (violent) content can have positive effects on emotional regulation and mood management (Bowman & Tamborini, 2015), such as reduced stress and positive mood. Taking the notion of process further, the next section will focus on 'how' to account for the extent to which behaviours around gaming (rather than on games and content themselves) are important in understanding the range of effects.

How

'How' here refers to the processes and behaviours surrounding gaming. Insights here could be gleaned from the literature on playfulness or other forms of gaming (e.g. board gaming), yet this is not a mainstream approach in the (cyber) psychological literature on gaming. Instead, a prominent debate in the psychology of digital gaming is that of excessive gaming (i.e. playing too much). Again, there is much controversy involved here, with some scholars liberally using terms such as 'Gaming Disorder' and 'Internet Gaming Disorder' (Petry, Rehbein, Gentile, Lemmens, Rumpf, Mößle et al., 2014; Rumpf, Achab, Billieux, Bowden-Jones, Carragher, Demetrovics et al., 2018), whilst others are more cautious in their approach (Griffiths, van Rooij, Kardefelt-Winther, Starcevic, Király, Pallesen, et al., 2016; van Rooij, Ferguson, Carras, Kardefelt-Winther, Shi, Aarseth, et al., 2018). Whilst I do not intend to scrutinise the 'gaming addiction' literature, I include this here as a way of illustrating how the effects of digital games can be influenced by the behaviours afforded to them. That is, gaming for prolonged periods of time whilst neglecting the functional aspects of life is not healthy and may result in a range of negative outcomes such as a sedentary lifestyle, poor psychosocial functioning, and maladaptive behaviours (Busch, Manders, & de Leeuw, 2013). The same could be said for any sedentary hobby or activity in fact. However, gaming behaviour is not just about the maladaptive end of the spectrum, despite it being the main focus of the academic literature and public debate.

Understanding the processes involved in gaming is important. For example, theoretical frameworks to understand gaming outcomes should account for the variety of factors involved and the process of gameplay itself (Kaye, 2017). This would include the nature of the gameplay session (e.g. whether it has been 'successful' or where dynamics with others have been positive) and the role of gaming as a form of enjoyable leisure-time activity, which may have equivalent regulatory benefits to other leisure pursuits (Kaye, 2017).

The effects of gaming may also be related to the investment in and commitment afforded to the activity, such as whether players are more 'hardcore' in their gaming behaviours or more 'casual'. Casual gaming typically involves playing 'easier' or 'lighter' games, often in short bursts on mobile or tablet devices, whereas hardcore players tend to play for longer, in uninterrupted sessions, and often on a console or PC (Eklund, 2016; Juul, 2010). Interestingly, mainstream debates about digital gaming tend to overlook the fact that these different gaming behaviours may have different effects.

Some research has explored the conceptual basis of gaming styles (Maher, Simon, & Winston, 2018), and how different playing styles such as casual vs. hardcore may elicit differences in enjoyment and fulfilment of intrinsic needs, with hardcore players often being more motivated by competence needs (Neys, Jansz, & Tan, 2014). Beyond this, it is unclear from the paucity of evidence how these different gaming behaviours correspond to the range of effects which have been observed in relation to digital games and gaming. It is more common for research in this area to take measures of 'gaming engagement' or 'gaming behaviour' simply by asking participants in surveys to report the number of hours they typically play per week or their gaming history. This information is then used to ascertain associations with psychological variables. However, these estimates of play time are by no means an adequate measure of gaming behaviour, especially given recent work showing that players' estimates of play time is not fully in line with their true play time, as revealed by log data (Johannes, Vuorre, & Przybylski, 2021). Therefore, a key recommendation of Johannes et al. (2021) is that researchers should collaborate with gaming companies through the use of ethical data sharing if we are to advance our understanding of the impact of gaming behaviours.

Why

Most people play games as an enjoyable and rewarding form of entertainment or leisure-time activity. Whilst this is undoubtedly the most common reason for playing, it is important to remember that games can also be played in serious or professional formats (Kaye, 2019). Serious games are those whose primary purpose is not for entertainment, but instead to engender positive effects such as promoting health, well-being, or training certain skills. These can include educational games, games for health, and training simulations. As well as serious gaming, there is also professional gaming such as e-Sports, a format of play that requires the same level of commitment and training as elite-level sport. Professional gaming is often viewed as a sport rather than play, and players are often referred to as athletes (Egliston, 2015; Jenny, Manning, Keiper, & Olrich, 2016).

Since function of play involves much more than simply playing for leisure, a key determinant of any effects associated with digital games and gaming will relate to their function. Whilst debates on the psychology of digital gaming do not tend to make explicit reference to the fact that they are exploring gaming for leisure, the majority of the existing literature has focused on this form of gaming. In respect of serious games, these tend to be explored outside the central debates in our field, often within the areas of educational technology (in the case of educational games) or digital health (for health and well-being games). Therefore, the many (largely positive) effects which are associated with playing these types of games are often missing from mainstream debates about the effects of games.

The types of effects of serious games depend entirely on their primary purpose. When used within education, some of these effects include: increased engagement in learning, positive attitudes to subject areas, increased subject knowledge, and motivation to learn (e.g. Dele-Ajayi, Sanderson, Strachan, & Pickard, 2016; Ge & Ifenthaler, 2018). In relation to physical health, the range of effects include: improved musculo-skeletal health, support with chronic conditions, physiotherapeutic benefits, and increased energy expenditure, to name but a few (Eichenberg & Schott, 2017; Holtz, Murray, & Park, 2018; Ingadottir, Jaarsma, & Klompstra, 2020). Also, serious games or 'digital games with a purpose' have also been used to support mental well-being, in cybersecurity and in industry, as well as in a wide range of other settings. It is beyond the scope of this chapter to outline all the observed effects, but the main point is that mainstream debates about the effects of digital games often overlook the serious functions of gaming. The same issue applies to eSports and other forms of professional gaming, as most of the existing literature relates to conceptualising eSports, spectatorship, cognitive or motor skills, and sports performance (Hamari & Sjöblom, 2017; van Hilvoorde & Pot, 2016; Zhuang, Yin, Zi, & Liu, 2020). However, perhaps this is appropriate based on the fact that eSports is best considered under the function of sport rather than play.

Where and who

As well as the 'what', 'how', and 'why' discussed previously, there is also the 'where' and 'who'. These will be discussed together as the main principles of these overlap somewhat. The development of games technology and internet connectivity means games can be played in a wide range of different places. It is no longer a case of 'same time, same place' for determining who players are able to play with, but rather 'anytime, anywhere'. This means that games can be played with others irrespective of where they are, opening up the possibility of playing not just with existing friends but with players from all over the world. Furthermore, the development of games technology that is increasingly mobile (e.g. tablets, smartphones) offers players a wider range of places to engage in gaming.

Research in the area of 'social gaming' has explored how the social setting of play, game task, and type of game partner relate to gaming effects. Social setting refers to whether someone is playing alone or in the presence of another, either virtually (online) or physically. Game task refers to whether the gaming task is cooperative or competitive in nature. And game partner, as one would expect, refers to who the other players are and the level of familiarity or closeness they have with you.

Largely these issues have been explored experimentally. To explore the impacts of social setting, participants are typically allocated a play condition where they either undertake a gaming task alone, while physically co-present with another player, or virtually mediated with another player. Findings typically show that there is a linear increase in intensity of effects across solo, virtually mediated, and physically co-present forms of play (for a review, see Kaye, 2021). This has been shown to be the case for physiological arousal, mood, and immersion. Findings generally suggest that playing with other people (particularly when physically present) enhances the psychological effects of gaming (Cairns, Cox, Day, Martin, & Perryman, 2013; Mandryk, Inkpen, & Calvert, 2006; Ravaja, 2009). For example, physical presence is related to greater perceptions of positive mood and social competence relative to virtual presence or playing alone (Gajadhar, de Kort, & IJsselsteijn, 2008; Powell & Kaye, 2018).

A similar approach has been adopted to explore type of gaming task and game partner. When comparing the physiological and psychological effects of cooperative vs. competitive types of gameplay, differences have been observed. Namely, competitive tasks tend to result in higher physiological arousal (Lim & Lee, 2009), whilst cooperative tasks are related to subsequent prosocial behaviours and favourable attitudes to others (Ewoldsen, Eno, Okdie, Velez, Guadagno, & DeCoster, 2012; Stiff & Kedra, 2020).

In addition to social setting and task type, research has explored whether it matters with whom you are playing. For example, Ravaja, Saari, Turpeinen, Laarni, Salminen, and Kivikangas (2006) compared the physiological and psychological effects between game conditions where participants either played against a friend, a stranger, or a computer. Findings showed that playing with a friend elicited greater physiological arousal and perceptions of presence and engagement compared with playing against a stranger. Correspondingly, other research has established the importance of gaming-related friendships and social circles in gaming (Domahidi, Festl, & Quandt, 2014; Kowert, Domahidi, Festl & Quandt, 2014).

So, like the 'what', 'how', and 'why', it is clear to see that the 'where' and 'who' are of paramount importance when theorising about the effects of digital gaming.

Conclusion

The mainstream psychological literature on the effects of digital games and gaming has largely focused on the 'what' and 'how'. Also, most literature has focused on one type of content (violence) and gaming behaviours that are at one end of the spectrum (excessive, problematic use). It is clear that the effects which games can have are much more varied than previously thought and a focus on the range of 'whats', 'hows', 'whys', 'wheres', and 'whos' is important for recognising these.

It would be most beneficial to move beyond a paradigm that views a linear path between gaming and effects. Looking at gaming in the context of being playful activity (e.g. board games) would not involve such a restrictive pathway of effects. Historical literature in this area, such as that on media violence effects, has largely rendered the playful pastime of digital gaming impervious to the same scrutiny. It is safe to say that the pathways between digital games and gaming are by no means linear (as shown in this chapter) and an 'effects' perspective is rather outdated and restrictive.

Box 9.2: Thinking activity

Consider you are playing a mobile game on your smartphone (e.g., Candy Crush, Angry Birds, Among Us):

- What might be different if you were instead to play a game on another platform (e.g. PC, console)?
- How might this be different psychologically?

Box 9.3: Take-home message

The effects of digital games and gaming are complex. To understand these more fully, we need to move away from talking about digital games and gaming, and instead understand effects through the lenses of what, how, why, who, and where, and how these interact with one another.

References

Ajzen, I. (1985). From intentions to actions: A theory of planned behavior. In J. Kuhl & J. Beckmann (Eds.), *Action control* (pp. 11–39). Berlin: Springer.

Ajzen, I. (1991). The theory of planned behavior. *Organizational Behavior and Human Decision Processes, 50* (2), 179–211. https://doi.org/10.1016/0749-5978(91)90020-T

Ajzen, I., & Madden, T.J. (1986). Prediction of goal-directed behavior: Attitudes, intentions, and perceived behavioral control. *Journal of Experimental Social Psychology, 22* (5), 453–474. https://doi.org/10.1016/0022-1031(86)90045-4

Anderson, C.A., Bushman, B.J., Bartholow, B.D., Cantor, J., Christakis, D., Coyne, S.M. et al. (2017). Screen violence and youth behavior. *Pediatrics, 140* (2), S142–S147. https://doi.org/10.1542/peds.2016-1758T

Anderson, C.A., Shibuya, A., Ihori, N., Swing, E.L., Bushman, B.J., Sakamoto, A. et al. (2010). Violent video game effects on aggression, empathy, and prosocial behavior in Eastern and Western countries. *Psychological Bulletin, 136* (2), 151–173. https://doi.org/10.1037/a0018251

Bowman, N.D., & Tamborini, R. (2015). 'In the mood to game': Selective exposure and mood management processes in computer game play. *New Media & Society, 17* (3), 375–393. https://doi.org/10.1177/1461444813504274

Busch, V., Manders, L.A., & de Leeuw, R.J. (2013). Screen time associated with health behaviors and outcomes in adolescents. *American Journal of Health Behavior, 37* (6), 819–830. https://doi.org/10.5993/AJHB.37.6.11

Cairns, P., Cox, A.L., Day, M., Martin, M., & Perryman, T. (2013). Who but not where: The effect of social play on immersion in digital games. *International Journal of Human-Computer Studies, 71* (11), 1069–1077. https://doi.org/10.1016/j.ijhcs.2013.08.015

DeLisi, M., Vaughn, M.G., Gentile, D.A., Anderson, C.A., & Shook, J. (2013). Violent video games, delinquency, and youth violence: New evidence. *Youth Violence and Juvenile Justice, 11,* 132–142. https://doi.org/10.1177/1541204012460874

Dele-Ajayi, O., Sanderson, J., Strachan, R., & Pickard, A. (2016). Learning mathematics through serious games: An engagement framework. Presentation to the *2016 IEEE Frontiers in Education Conference (FIE)*, Erie, PA. https://doi.org/10.1109/FIE.2016.7757401

Domahidi, E., Festl, R., & Quandt, T. (2014). To dwell among gamers: Investigating the relationship between social online game use and gaming-related friendships. *Computers in Human Behavior, 35,* 107–115. https://doi.org/10.1016/j.chb.2014.02.023

Eichenberg, C., & Schott, M. (2017). Serious games for psychotherapy: A systematic review. *Games for Health Journal, 6* (3), 127–135. https://doi.org/10.1089/g4h.2016.0068

Egliston, B. (2015). Playing across media: Exploring transtextuality in competitive games and eSports. In *Proceedings of DiGRA 2015: Diversity of Play: Games, Cultures, Identities.* Retrieved 26 July 2017 from: http://www.digra.org/wp-content/uploads/digital-library/122_Egliston_Playing-Across-Media.pdf

Eklund, L. (2016). Who are the casual gamers? Gender tropes and tokenism in game culture. In T. Leaver & M. Willson (Eds.), *Social, casual and mobile games: The changing gaming landscape* (pp. 15–29). London: Bloomsbury Academic.

Elson, M., & Ferguson, C.J. (2014). Twenty-five years of research on violence in digital games and aggression: Empirical evidence, perspectives, and a debate gone astray. *European Psychologist, 19* (1), 33–46. https://doi.org/10.1027/1016-9040/a000147

Ewoldsen, D.R., Eno, C.A., Okdie, B.M., Velez, J.A., Guadagno, R.E., & DeCoster, J. (2012). Effect of playing violent video games cooperatively or competitively on subsequent cooperative behavior. *Cyberpsychology, Behavior, and Social Networking, 15,* 277–280. https://doi.org/10.1089/cyber.2011.0308

Ferguson, C.J. (2015). Do angry birds make for angry children? A meta-analysis of video game influences on children's and adolescents' aggression, mental health, prosocial behavior, and academic performance. *Perspectives in Psychological Science, 10* (5), 646–666. https://doi.org/10.1177/1745691615592234

Gajadhar, B.J., de Kort, Y.A.W., & IJsselsteijn, W.A. (2008). Shared fun is doubled fun: Player enjoyment as a function of social setting. In P. Markopoulos, B. de Ruyter, W. IJsselsteijn, & D. Rowland (Eds.), *Fun and games* (pp. 106–117). New York: Springer.

Ge, X., & Ifenthaler, D. (2018). Designing engaging educational games and assessing engagement in game-based learning. In M. Khosrow-Pour (Ed.), *Gamification in education: Breakthroughs in research and practice* (pp. 1–9). Hershey, PA: IGI Global.

Green, C.S., & Bavelier, D. (2003). Action video game modifies visual selective attention. *Nature, 423*, 534–537. https://doi.org/10.1038/nature01647

Green, C.S., & Bavelier, D. (2006). Effect of action video games on the spatial distribution of visuospatial attention. *Journal of Experimental Psychology, 32* (6), 1465–1478. https://doi.org/10.1037/0096-1523.32.6.1465

Green, C.S., & Bavelier, D. (2007). Action-video game experience alters the spatial resolution of vision. *Psychological Science, 18* (1), 88–94. https://doi.org/10.1111/j.1467-9280.2007.01853.x

Greitemeyer, T., & Osswald, S. (2010). Effects of prosocial video games on prosocial behavior. *Journal of Personality and Social Psychology, 98* (2), 211–221. https://doi.org/10.1037/a0016997

Griffiths M.D., Van Rooij, A.J., Kardefelt-Winther D., Starcevic, V., Király, O., Pallesen, S. et al. (2016). Working towards an international consensus on criteria for assessing internet gaming disorder: A critical commentary on Petry et al. (2014). *Addiction, 111* (1), 167–175. https://doi.org/10.1111/add.13057

Hamari, J., & Sjöblom, M. (2017). What is eSports and why do people watch it? *Internet Research, 27* (2), 211–232. https://doi.org/10.1108/IntR-04-2016-0085

Holtz, B.E., Murray, K., & Park, T. (2018). Serious games for children with chronic diseases: A systematic review. *Games for Health Journal, 7* (5), 291–301. http://doi.org/10.1089/g4h.2018.0024

Ingadottir, B., Jaarsma, T., & Klompstra, L. (2020). Let the games begin: Serious games in prevention and rehabilitation to improve outcomes in patients with cardiovascular disease. *European Journal of Cardiovascular Nursing, 19* (7), 558–560. https://doi.org/10.1177/1474515120934058

Jenny, S.E., Manning, R.D., Keiper, M.C., & Olrich, T.W. (2016). Virtual(ly) athletes: Where eSports fit within the definition of 'sport'. *Quest, 69* (1), 1–18. https://doi.org/10.1080/00336297.2016.1144517

Johannes, N., Vuorre, M., & Przybylski, A.K. (2021). Video game play is positively correlated with well-being. *Royal Society Open Science, 8* (2), 202049. https://doi.org/10.1098/rsos.202049

Juul, J. (2010). *A casual revolution: Reinvesting video games and their players.* Cambridge, MA: MIT Press.

Kaye, L.K. (2017). The process model of gameplay to understand digital gaming outcomes. In M. Khosrow-Pour (Ed.), *Encyclopedia of information science and technology*, 4th edition (pp. 3317–3326). Hershey, PA: IGI Global.

Kaye, L.K. (2019). Gaming classifications and player demographics. In A. Attrill-Smith, C. Fullwood, M. Keep, & D.J. Kuss (Eds.), *Oxford handbook of cyberpsychology* (pp. 609–626). Oxford: Oxford University Press.

Kaye, L.K. (2021). Understanding the 'social' nature of digital games. *Entertainment Computing, 38*, 100420. https://doi.org/10.1016/j.entcom.2021.100420

Kowert, R., Domahidi, E., Festl, R., & Quandt, T. (2014). Social gaming, lonely life?: The impact of digital game play on adolescents' social circles. *Computers in Human Behavior, 36*, 385–390. https://doi.org/10.1016/j.chb.2014.04.003

Lim, S., & Lee, J.R. (2009). When playing together feels different: Effects of task types and social contexts on physiological arousal in multiplayer online gaming contexts. *CyberPsychology & Behavior, 12* (1), 59–61. https://doi.org/10.1089/cpb.2008.0054

Maher, H., Simon, M.A., & Winston, C.N. (2018). What's your style? Preliminary validation of the Gaming Styles Questionnaire. *Journal of Creativity in Mental Health, 13* (2), 159–168. https://doi.org/10.1080/15401383.2017.1342581

Mandryk, R., Inkpen, K.M., & Calvert, T.W. (2006). Using psychophysiological techniques to measure user experience with entertainment technologies. *Behaviour and Information Technology, 25* (2), 141–158. https://doi.org/10.1080/01449290500331156

McCain, J., Morrison, K., & Ahn, S.J. (2019). Video games and behavior change. In A. Atrill-Smith, C. Fullwood, M. Keep, & D.J. Kuss (Eds.), *The Oxford handbook of cyberpsychology* (pp. 509–531). Oxford: Oxford University Press.

Michie, S., van Stralen, M.M., & West, R. (2011). The behaviour change wheel: A new method for characterising and designing behaviour change interventions. *Implementation Science, 6*, 42. https://doi.org/10.1186/1748-5908-6-42

Neys, J.L.D., Jansz, J., & Tan, E.S.H. (2014). Exploring persistence in gaming: The role of self-determination and social identity. *Computers in Human Behavior, 37*, 196–209. https://doi.org/10.1016/j.chb.2014.04.047

Petry, N.M., Rehbein, F., Gentile, D.A., Lemmens, J.S., Rumpf, H.J., Mößle, T. et al. (2014). An international consensus for assessing internet gaming disorder using the new DSM-5 approach. *Addiction, 109*, 1399–1406. https://doi.org/10.1111/add.12457

Powell, J., & Kaye, L.K. (2018). The effect of physical co-location on social competence, gaming engagement and gamer identity within a competitive multiplayer game. *Open Science Journal of Psychology, 5* (4), 38–44. http://www.openscienceonline.com/journal/archive2?journalId=740&paperId=4586

Ravaja, N. (2009). The psychophysiology of digital gaming: The effect of a non-co-located opponent. *Media Psychology, 12* (3), 268–294. https://doi.org/10.1080/15213260903052240

Ravaja, N., Saari, T., Turpeinen, M., Laarni, J., Salminen, M., & Kivikangas, M. (2006). Spatial presence and emotions during video game playing: Does it matter with whom you play? *Presence: Teleoperators and Virtual Environments, 15* (4), 381–392. https://doi.org/10.1162/pres.15.4.381

Rumpf, H.J., Achab, S., Billieux, J., Bowden-Jones, H., Carragher, N., Demetrovics, Z. et al. (2018). Including gaming disorder in the ICD-11: The need to do so from a clinical and public health perspective. Commentary on: A weak scientific basis for gaming disorder: Let us err on the side of caution (van Rooij et al., 2018). *Journal of Behavioral Addiction, 7* (3), 556–561. https://doi.org/10.1556/2006.7.2018.59

Stiff, C., & Bowen, T. (2016). Two-player game: Playing casual video games with outgroup members reduces levels of prejudice toward that outgroup. *International Journal of Human-Computer Interaction, 32* (12), 912–920. httpS://doi.org/10.1080/10447318.2016.1212484

Stiff, C., & Kedra, P. (2020). Playing well with others: The role of opponent and intergroup anxiety in the reduction of prejudice through collaborative video game play. *Psychology of Popular Media, 9* (1), 105–115. https://doi.org/10.1037/ppm0000210

Van Hilvoorde, I., & Pot, N. (2016). Embodiment and fundamental motor skills in eSports. *Sport, Ethics and Philosophy, 10* (1), 14–27. https://doi.org/10.1080/17511321.2016.1159246

Van Rooij, A.J., Ferguson, C., Carras, M.C., Kardefelt-Winther, D., Shi, J., Aarseth, E. et al. (2018). A weak scientific basis for gaming disorder: Let us err on the side of caution. *Journal of Behavioral Addiction, 7* (1), 1–9. https://doi.org/10.1556/2006.7.2018.19

Zhuang, W., Yin, K., Zi, Y., & Liu, Y. (2020). Non-invasive brain stimulation: Augmenting the training and performance potential in eSports players. *Brain Sciences, 10* (7), 454. https://doi.org/10.3390/brainsci10070454

PART 4

Society

10 Using online data

In twenty-first-century Western society, data is imperative for a range of economical, educational, security, legal, and commercial purposes. Every time we use an internet search engine, we contribute a data source that often includes a range of associated metadata, thus adding to a vast compendium of server data. This not only helps to build a profile of individual users but also contributes to understanding societal patterns more generally. In basic terms, data is evidence of behaviour having taken place, which, from a cyberpsychological perspective, is a fruitful opportunity to explore human behaviour in the digital age. It is somewhat surprising, therefore, that cyberpsychology researchers have made limited use of such data, notwithstanding the methodological, security, and privacy challenges this may entail. A notable exception, however, is the Human Screenome project (for an overview, see Reeves, Robinson, & Ram, 2020), which unobtrusively collected users' screen recordings, showing moment-by-moment changes on users' screens. However, the research resources from this project are not freely available to allow other researchers to take advantage of these methods, creating barriers to making progress in such endeavours.

The following sections will discuss the range of uses of online data, and how these can be particularly useful in helping us understand and benefit twenty-first-century society.

What do we mean by online data?

Online data can refer to information which users themselves provide explicitly or, in some cases, not so explicitly. Examples of explicit data-giving include users registering with a website or completing fields in an online form. As a part of this, users typically confirm their agreement to a set of terms and conditions about how their data will be stored and used. However, there are also less explicit forms of online data from users. These cover a range of things users do online, such as the webpages they visit, the content they interact with, and the contacts they connect with via social networking sites. This sort of information is collected both by the specific sites they visit as well as more general internet service providers. Additionally, metadata is also collected from both of these types of data-giving processes. Metadata includes the type of browser being used, IP address, geolocation, time and date of comments being posted, and so on. These activities are often discussed in terms of active vs. passive digital footprints, where 'active' refers to the traceable digital activities that are actioned deliberately by an individual, and 'passive' relates to the more subtle behaviours of users such as web-browsing.

There are two issues to note here with regards to user consent. The first is consent to this data being *collected* in the first place, and the second how it is *used* – it is the latter that forms the basis for this chapter. Much of this data will be of the not-so-explicit type. This data is then processed using such techniques as data scraping, or by automated algorithmic systems. No matter how this data is processed, there are ethical and privacy considerations in relation to how it is used to make inferences about both individuals and society.

Before exploring some of the prominent uses of online data, it is enlightening to consider everyday behaviour more generally. When we give away our online data, we are not only providing third-party information about our *online* behaviour – far from it. In a world that is increasingly part of an 'Internet of Things' (IoT) network, where many of our objects are internet-enabled and -connected, more and more information can be collected and stored about our everyday movements, much of it having nothing to with being online. The IoT involves a range of objects, including wearables (e.g. smartwatches), virtual assistants (e.g. Alexa), smart home security systems (e.g. video doorbells), and smart connected appliances (e.g. smart washing machines or dishwashers). Anyone who possesses these devices is part of that network, providing insights into their behaviour and everyday movements. So, it is not simply 'online data' that we are giving away, but data about our behaviours more generally.

Furthermore, being so hyper-connected likely means that it is not just the individual user who is affected. For example, smart baby monitors provide data that is revealing of another party – in this case, someone who cannot provide consent. Similarly, the introduction of wearables (e.g. GPS trackers and temperature sensors) for pets and farm animals for the purposes of tracking, monitoring, and controlling has given rise to an 'Internet of Animals' movement (van der Linden, Edwards, Hadar, & Zamansky, 2020). Thus it is important to remember that whilst all these connected devices are designed for pragmatic, gainful purposes, the impact of technology use extends beyond the individual user to other parties – indeed, other species. The remainder of this chapter, however, will focus on human uses, given this is perhaps the most pressing concern.

Legal uses

There are a number of ways in which online data has legal uses and implications. A major legal component that constrains how online data can be used relates to data protection regulations. This refers to the extent to which data collected about people is kept secure and private, and is used lawfully. In the European Union (EU), this is regulated by the General Data Protection Regulation (GDPR), and for UK organisations sits alongside the Data Protection Act (2018). This is especially relevant in relation to personal and identifiable information, in that organisations are legally obliged to put in place appropriate measures to protect such information. A further aspect of this concerns minors and the age of digital consent, which, in many nations, is set at 13 years, but can be up to 16 years. This relates to the minimum age at which online service providers are legally allowed to use a minor's personal data based on that minor's own consent. The use of data of anyone under the age of digital consent requires the consent of a parent or guardian.

The age of digital consent, however, is difficult to regulate. Users can sign up to websites or online accounts, many of which do not ask for date of birth information. Even those that do ask for proof of age do not require verification on the part of the user. Similarly, minors can use their parents' account details to access online platforms, meaning their data in a sense could be used inadvertently because it is assumed to be that of an adult. Parents can also register with a service that is primarily designed for their child, such as 'Pickatale', an online interactive storybook platform. Here, the data collected from the behaviours tracked on the platform (e.g. books read, quiz results, reading progress reports) would be that of the child, not the parent, even though the parent was the registered user. And it is not only the platform itself which collects and uses children's data, but also a range of third-party data processors such as Google, Microsoft, and Amazon. In such cases, how the age of digital consent legislation applies is unclear.

Notwithstanding data protection legislation, there are potential legal issues relating to online data. Smart devices such as voice-activated home assistants (e.g. Amazon's Echo or Alexa) and smartphone voice assistants (Apple's Siri) have come under the spotlight due to claims they inconspicuously garner unauthorised voice data/recordings from users. However, data from devices such as these can be used as part of legal proceedings – audio recordings, for example, may be used as evidence in the prosecution of a crime, in that they may provide audio evidence of domestic violence, child abuse, or a burglary. In one court case in the US, the judge requested audio recording data from an Amazon Echo device so that it could be used as evidence in a murder case. However, this has prompted substantial debate surrounding data privacy and whether the utility of such data to support the judicial process outweighs user privacy rights.

Just as smart device recordings can be used as circumstantial evidence of an alleged crime, other types of online data can be used as evidence of criminal intent. For example, criminal proceedings have made use of online correspondence that includes weapon emoji (e.g. knives, pistols) as evidence that the sender intended 'real threat'. In other cases, prosecutors have successfully argued that a defendant's use of an emoji with 'Xs' for eyes alongside the name of the victim was evidence of premediated murder. These cases raise some interesting questions around user privacy and the extent to which 'private' online data use in legal proceedings overrides the user's right for privacy.

Security, surveillance, and protection uses

Another context in which users' right to privacy may arguably be a secondary consideration is that of public protection as part of national defence, safety, and security. This includes surveillance (e.g. threat detection), equipment tracking, public infrastructure (e.g. law enforcement), and the emergency services (e.g. homeland security, border security) (Fraga-Lamas, Fernández-Caramés, Suárez-Albela, Castedo, & González-López, 2016). In relation to surveillance, insider threat detection and prediction is one area that has benefited substantially from the monitoring of online data. For example, log files of online systems (e.g. daily log-ons to files accessed, email transactions, web server logs) and social media websites are commonly used to enable threat detection in organisations (Gheyas & Abdallah, 2016).

Cybersecurity is dedicated to data protection and security and can take a variety of different forms. These include operational security (processes for handling data assets), information security (protecting privacy and integrity of data), and application security (protecting software and hardware from threats to make them vulnerable). These sorts of security are operationalised using both system-level protections such as anti-virus software, and individual-level strategies such as using strong passwords and avoiding public WiFi. These are ways individuals and organisations can use make good use of cybersecurity principles to protect their own and others' data.

Humans are often viewed as the 'weak link' when it comes to cybersecurity, whereby human error or ignorance is responsible for compromises in security. However, it is also the case that humans can be the solution to cybersecurity problems, in that user engagement (especially in the context of employees in businesses) is central to cybersecurity efforts (Zimmermann & Renaud, 2019). This typically involves employee training in cybersecurity, which often is generic in nature, such as how to spot a phishing email. However, this does not ameliorate the many reasons underpinning people's cybersecurity practices (or lack thereof), which range from poor IT literacy and general reluctance to misattribution of one's responsibility. To optimise the human element of cybersecurity in businesses, personalised training is paramount to ensure fuller and more effective engagement by users.

In contrast to its surveillance uses in the context of defence and security, online data also has the potential to be used for monitoring employee productivity and performance. For example, Microsoft's productivity score has been criticised as being a tool for workplace surveillance whereby employee productivity is monitored at an individual level. This involves using data about communications, meetings, content collaboration, and teamwork across the range of Microsoft 365 products (*The Guardian*, 2020). For obvious reasons, such analytic tools have been met with criticism and concern, largely in respect of employee privacy.

In terms of public health protection, the Covid-19 pandemic has highlighted how smartphone apps can be used to gather data about users' location and proximity to other users as part of contact tracing protocols. Similarly, health passes or vaccine passports have been mooted, whereby medical data could be used to verify whether an individual has been immunised, thus allowing them to use the services of entertainment vendors such as Ticketmaster, or be permitted to travel internationally. In the context of Covid-19 vaccination, therefore, the way this sort of data could be used has implications not only for public health protection but other sectors and services as well. Both in respect of public health and national security, using people's (private) online data argu- ably supersedes one's right to privacy but only if this data is collected and used in accordance with data protection regulations and, in the case of a security breach, in line with principles around reporting to other relevant authorities.

Educational uses

There are a number of opportunities for using online data for educational pur- poses. A rather controversial example from the summer of 2020 in the UK was the proposal that school leavers' final subject results be calculated based on an algorithm. At the time, A-level[1] students were not able to sit their final exams due to the Covid-19 pandemic. Rather than rely on teacher-assessed grades, which were deemed too biased, unstandardised, and liable to inflation, the edu- cation regulator, Ofqual, proposed using an algorithm. For any given student, their grades were to be calculated based on their school's historical grade data and their teachers' rankings of their perceived performance relative to their peers. However, it was considered by many that the results based on this algo- rithm would not only be inaccurate (in many cases significantly lower than expected) but also disadvantage certain students. Based on this widespread criticism, the approach was ditched in favour of teacher-assessed grades.

This is an interesting example because it highlights the legalities around using an algorithm to make decisions and profile individuals. Specifically, it was argued that automating decisions about individual students based on his- torical aggregate data potentially violated GDPR principles. That is, data protection law requires the fair and transparent use of data in algorithms, and that the use of an algorithm does not result in unfair or discriminatory out- comes. Had such an algorithm been better able to attend to individual-level performance data and other relevant data, it may have been seen to be a more efficacious tool for educational purposes.

Another recent controversial example is that of online proctoring software to provide surveillance of students as they perform exams at home. This requires students to enable their webcam and to provide a 360° sweep of the room they are occupying to verify they are not obtaining external help with their exams. The software continues to track them as they take their exam. This form of exam invigilation has come under close scrutiny, especially in light of its use to monitor remote study during the Covid-19 pandemic. Although a useful authentication tool, this use of online data clearly has serious implications for user privacy, perceptions of safety, and issues related to safe- guarding, and there have been calls for it to be banned.

'Educational' uses do not relate solely to formal education, since data can also be used for AI purposes and machine learning by teaching systems how to make accurate predictions about subsequent data by inputting training sets of data. For example, in China, 'Infervision' uses AI and deep learning to support radiologists to diagnose cancer from CT scans. Infervision is trained based on real-life lung scan data and taught algorithms to help identify signs of cancerous growths on lung scans. In addition, personal data can be used for adaptive education, whereby course content is personalised based on learner needs, and content is generated based on past behaviours. This would be powered by an AI training programme that generates learning insights from learner behaviour, helping it predict and be responsive to learners' progression. This data-driven approach could be a significant advance for online and distance education provision.

Clearly, some of these examples have merit in relation to the societal benefits they may bring, in that user data may be both beneficial to oneself (in the personalised learning example) and to others (in the Infervision example). However, these do pose a threat to the need for human intervention. The debate around jobs for the future raises questions about how AI may replace the human taskforce, contributing to increased unemployment and poorer career prospects. That being said, many of the ways in which AI and machine learning work rely largely on supervised methods where humans train and oversee the process, which may reassure some that the robots are not yet ready to take over!

Economical and commercial uses

With the benefits of digitalisation, online data can provide a means of automating many services and systems, thus reducing the need for human input and potential biases. One such example is independent online loan companies, which use a plethora of online data to determine the trustworthiness of loan applicants to inform loan decisions. Online data here refers to many things, but include metadata such as geolocation, which can signal how stable someone's home and job situation may be, data from user devices such as clicks and key strokes to help verify if the online applicant is a human, and external data such as number of connections on LinkedIn (Hegarty & Damelin, 2015). Algorithms which automate the process for online loan decisions based on an automatic trustworthiness protocol therefore ensure speedy loan decisions and reduce any potential for human bias in the process. Similarly, companies such as PayPal use systems to screen online payments and corroborate users' personal data (e.g. browser information, IP addresses) as a way of improving user trust in online financial exchanges.

From an economic perspective, the use of online data, particularly when collected over a period of time, can be especially useful. For example, scraping data from online retail sites enables prices and the levels of inflation to be monitored (Cavallo, 2011). Another example involves retrieving data across multiple sources to garner information about product recommendations (Bhattacharjee, Gopal, Lertwachara, & Marsden, 2006), which can help tailor recommendation algorithms, thus boosting commercial gain. Similarly, data such as product reviews and comments from social media sites can also be scraped from the internet as a means of understanding consumer preferences and behaviour, to inform future commercial strategies.

Political uses

Online data, usually in the form of social media data, is becoming increasingly relevant in the political context. A good example of this is the infamous Facebook-Cambridge Analytica scandal, in which Facebook users' personal data was used by Cambridge Analytica, without their consent, for the purposes of political advertising. Despite the widespread outcry and publicity afforded to this scandal, an investigation did not identify any cases of data misuse and the enquiry concluded that the methods used were commonly adopted. Indeed, political parties have always made use of people's personal data as part of the campaign process, although there have been calls recently for better regulation to help ensure transparency in how personal data is used (ICO, 2020). A recent example in Washington, DC illustrates this issue, in which it was claimed that churchgoers had been tracked based on their geolocation data from their smartphones by political action groups. Specifically, it was claimed that the data was used to connect with Catholics, to encourage them to register to vote and go to the polls. This process is known as 'geo-fencing', where people's frequently visited places are identified to allow marketers to tailor their advertising of goods or services to them, in this case, to encourage political engagement.

It has also been highlighted how social media sites, including Facebook, played a role in amplifying false and misleading content relating to the 2020 US Presidential election, and that the around two-thirds of people who joined extremist or far-right political Facebook groups did so because of the algorithms which recommended them to do so. It is clear, then, that users' data is being fed into algorithms which threaten the democratic process.

Research uses

As well as the range of uses outlined above, researchers may use online data to understand human behaviour. Within cyberpsychology, this is often referred to as 'internet-mediated research' (IMR), which can take two forms: reactive and non-reactive. Reactive forms of IMR include developing online surveys and doing online interviews, where participants actively engage with some form of research instrument or process. The focus of this section, however, is on non-reactive forms of IMR. This is where (public) online data is unobtrusively gathered and analysed to make inferences about human behaviour. Within psychology, both these approaches have to follow strict ethical standards. The main distinction with non-reactive approaches is that participants are not actively signing up to the research, and so no consent process is involved. The caveat here is that researchers should only use public data (i.e. that is publicly accessible, not behind authentication, etc.) (BPS, 2021).

There are different ways researchers can obtain and process online data for research purposes. This often involves some form of data scraping and extraction process, most likely using relevant software. Software can vary in complexity, some of which requires coding expertise in Python or R to write a script to run a scrape of the (text-based) data. Other software involves pre-designed searches that do not require coding knowledge for researchers to use. Some good examples of these are 'Laurence Anthony's FireAnt' (Filter, Identify, Report, and Export Analysis Toolkit). This is a freeware social media and data analysis toolkit with built-in visualisation tools, including time-series, geo-position, and network plotting. Another is 'Phantom Buster', which runs code-free automations and data extraction. Finally, 'DiscoverText' is a widely used tool in academic research to collect, clean, and analyse text data.

Irrespective of the software used to extract online data, the data can be collected in one of two ways: retrospectively (of historical data) or in real time. However, historical online data is becoming increasingly difficult to obtain, particularly as most commercial software tends to have, at the very most, a maximum history limit of 7 days from current day. Previously, researchers might have made use of Twitter data and used Twitter's API (Application Programming Interface) to extract such data. However, this has recently become more restricted and most typically the only way to gain historical data from Twitter is via requests from Twitter archives, which entail a fee. Recently, however, Twitter developers have acknowledged the restrictions this places on researchers and it has developed a new Twitter API which is designed specifically with researchers in mind (Tornes & Trujillo, 2021).

The alternative to using historical data is to gather real-time data, which all of the previously outlined software is set up to do. This can help researchers scrape data by research enquiry, such as hashtags, keywords, user/timeline, metadata (geo-location, user, time posted, etc.). Researchers can simply set the time period they wish the software to auto-run its search and generate an exportable text file with search results that can be processed.

The research uses outlined here are considered ethically appropriate by professional organisations in psychology and associated disciplines (BPS, 2021; Franzke, Bechmann, Zimmer, Ess et al., 2020). However, one approach that is not typically considered ethically sound is that of manipulating users' online experiences without informed consent and using subsequent online data to making inferences about the causal effects of these manipulations. This is exactly the strategy which underpinned the infamous Facebook Mood Manipulation experiment, in which researchers manipulated around 700,000 Facebook users' newsfeeds (Kramer, Guillory, & Hancock, 2014; see also editorial concerns from Verma, 2014). Some users were manipulated to be exposed to positive content and others negative content. It was subsequently revealed that manipulated users were more likely to post content that was congruent with the type of content they had been exposed to previously. The lack of informed consent as well as the mood-inducing manipulation that underpinned this research is of significant concern, and raises additional questions about the practical significance of the findings. For example, if social technology companies are equipped with these findings, how may the principles of such manipulation be used in the future to exploit users? Clearly, this is a good example of the dangers of how online data could be used for research, but also shows how our online data can be revealing of interesting individual and societal level psychological processes.

A final point to note about using online data for research purposes relates to its potential value in improving standards of data quality and scientific methods of enquiry. This is important in light of the 'replication crisis' evident in psychology and other scientific disciplines (Open Science Collaboration, 2015; Stanley, Carter, & Doucouliagos, 2018). This largely relates to how many existing findings in science are not sufficiently replicable, which has been attributed, at least in part, to exploiting flexibility in data collection, analysis, and reporting. However, making use of objective behavioural data, often in very large quantities, is a significant opportunity for researchers to address some of the limitations of existing research paradigms. For example, previous research has made exemplary use of big datasets from online gaming platforms to explore issues such as skill acquisition and priming effects (Stafford, 2018; Stafford & Dewar, 2014), the latter of which would be a particularly good candidate for scrutiny in the replication crisis. As such, (big) online datasets which can enhance the objectivity of behavioural measures represent a good opportunity for researchers.

Conclusion

A vast array of uses of online data can be used to serve many areas of twenty-first-century society. This data in some cases may reveal traces, identify patterns, and in some cases predict the behaviour of individuals themselves, and sometimes societally more generally. In all cases, there are key privacy and security considerations that need to be balanced against any potential benefits to society.

Box 10.1: Thinking activity

- List as many examples as you can of when you have given explicit consent for a company to collect and/or use your online data.
- List as many examples as you can of when you have provided a company with online data but you were unsure how this data might be used.

Box 10.2: Take-home message

Online data refers to many things and is involved in almost all aspects of everyday Western digital society. Whilst some data is given and used with explicit consent, there are a wide range of cases where user permission is less apparent, which raises important privacy considerations. Additionally, we have to remember that 'online data' also is increasingly mapping onto behaviours which do not occur exclusively online.

Note

1 A-level refers to Advanced Level in the UK national curriculum. Students aged 16–18 years complete this qualification over the course of two years (in sixth form or college), which is largely assessed by a set of final exams at the end of this period. In the context of the Covid-19 pandemic, these exams could not be completed and therefore the education regulator, Ofqual, was asked to intervene.

References

Bhattacharjee, S., Gopal, R.D., Lertwachara, K., & Marsden, J.R. (2006). Impact of legal threats on online music sharing activity: An analysis of music industry legal actions. *Journal of Law and Economics, 49* (1), 91–114. https://doi.org/10.2139/ssrn.816704

British Psychological Society (BPS) (2021). *Ethics guidelines for Internet-mediated research.* Leicester: BPS.

Cavallo, A. (2011). *Scraped data and sticky prices.* Retrieved 22 November 2020 from: https://www.nber.org/system/files/working_papers/w21490/w21490.pdf

Fraga-Lamas, P., Fernández-Caramés, T., Suárez-Albela, M., Castedo, L., & González-López, M.A. (2016). Review on Internet of things for defense and public safety. *Sensors, 16* (10), 1644. https://doi.org/10.3390/s16101644

Franzke, A.S., Bechmann, A., Zimmer, M., Ess, C., & the Association of Internet Researchers (2020). *Internet research: Ethical guidelines 3.0.* Retrieved 6 November 2020 from: https://aoir.org/reports/ethics3.pdf

Gheyas, I.A., & Abdallah, A.E. (2016). Detection and prediction of insider threats to cyber security: A systematic literature review and meta-analysis. *Big Data Analytics, 1,* 6. https://doi.org/10.1186/s41044-016-0006-0

Hegarty, D., & Damelin, E. (2015). U.S. Patent No. 2015/0278941 A1. Washington, DC: US Patent and Trademark Office.

Information Commissioner's Office (ICO) (2020) *Audits of data protection compliance by UK political parties: Summary report.* Retrieved 6 January 2021 from: https://ico.org.uk/media/action-weve-taken/2618567/audits-of-data-protection-compliance-by-uk-political-parties-summary-report.pdf

Kramer, A.D.I., Guillory, J.E., & Hancock, J.T. (2014). Experimental evidence of massive-scale emotional contagion through social networks. *Proceedings of the National Academy of Sciences USA, 111* (24), 8788–8790. https://doi.org/10.1073/pnas.1320040111

Open Science Collaboration (2015). Estimating the reproducibility of psychological science. *Science, 349* (6251), aac4716. https://doi.org/10.1126/science.aac4716

Reeves, B., Robinson, T., & Ram, N. (2020). Time for the Human Screenome Project. *Nature, 577,* 314–317. https://doi.org/10.1038/d41586-020-00032-5

Stafford, T. (2018). Female chess players outperform expectations when playing men. *Psychological Science, 29* (3), 429–436. https://doi.org/10.1177/0956797617736887

Stafford, T., & Dewar, M. (2014). Tracing the trajectory of skill learning with a very large sample of online game players. *Psychological Science, 25* (2), 511–518. https://doi.org/10.1177/0956797613511466

Stanley, T.D., Carter, E.C., & Doucouliagos, H. (2018). What meta-analyses reveal about the replicability of psychological research. *Psychological Bulletin, 144* (12), 1325–1346. https://doi.org/10.1037/bul0000169

The Guardian (2020). *Microsoft productivity score feature criticised as workplace surveillance.* Retrieved 15 February 2021 from: https://amp.theguardian.com/technology/2020/nov/26/microsoft-productivity-score-feature-criticised-workplace-surveillance?CMP=Share_iOSApp_Other&__twitter_impression=true

Tornes, A., & Trujillo, L. (2021). *Enabling the future of academic research with the Twitter API.* Retrieved 15 February 2021 from: https://blog.twitter.com/developer/en_us/topics/tools/2021/enabling-the-future-of-academic-research-with-the-twitter-api.html

van der Linden, D., Edwards, M., Hadar, I., & Zamansky, A. (2020). Pets without PETs: On pet owners' under-estimation of privacy concerns in pet wearables. *Proceedings on Privacy Enhancing Technologies (PoPETs), 2020* (1), 143–164. https://doi.org/10.2478/popets-2020-0009

Verma, I.M. (2014). Editorial expression of concern: Experimental evidence of massive-scale emotional contagion through social networks. *Proceedings of the National Academy of Sciences USA, 111* (29), 10779. https://doi.org/10.1073/pnas.1412469111

Zimmermann, V., & Renaud, K. (2019). Moving from a 'human-as-problem' to a 'human-as-solution' cybersecurity mindset. *International Journal of Human-Computer Studies, 131,* 169–187. https://doi.org/10.1016/j.ijhcs.2019.05.005

11 Cyberpsychology in the world

Cyberpsychology is a fast developing field and it is exciting to see more research and researchers being integrated into its thriving community. However, it is important to recognise that it also has an important role outside of academia, since many of the issues it addresses are a part of current public debate and are of societal concern. Cyberpsychology, therefore, has a key role in informing these debates as well as contributing to policy and practice. The chapter will outline some key areas where this is especially pertinent and provide examples of where academic, public, and policy considerations come together. It will conclude with some practical examples and a case study to illustrate how cyberpsychology research underpins research impact activities.

Media and public debate

Arguably, one of the main contributions of cyberpsychology is to inform the mass media and public debate. Over the last decade, there has been a significant increase in the coverage of technologies and the internet by the media, particularly in raising concerns about harms and threats to well-being associated with social media. However, similar concerns have been raised about 'screen-time', the 'addictive' properties of smartphones, and social media and digital gaming. Interestingly, in periods of lockdown during the Covid-19 pandemic, when many of us have been reliant on these platforms for fulfilling everyday life tasks, there has been more coverage of the benefits and value of social technologies.

The media has a critical role to play in raising awareness and informing public debate. A recent example involves a major British broadcasting company that employed a dedicated correspondent for (online) 'misinformation', highlighting that media companies can forge new pathways to help ensure such issues receive the exposure they deserve. However, researchers working in the field also have responsibilities. In particular, they should be mindful of the need for openness and transparency when reporting their findings, especially if the research is publicly funded. There are several ways in which cyberpsychology research can be disseminated to the media and public, some of which I outline below.

Open research practices

These include more formally recognised practices such as best practices in Open Science (e.g. pre-registering research protocols, making data available, sharing pre-prints), as well as a range of other more creative approaches, such as creating blog-posts, Tweet threads, animations, or YouTube vlogs/videos. All of these provide for a more accessible and public-facing approach to disseminating key research findings. These more creative approaches can help resolve four issues that threaten research accessibility:

- Financial barriers from academic journal paywalls
- Language barriers of academic jargon and style
- Time barriers whereby possible beneficiaries may not have sufficient time or resources to read academic literature
- Faster-paced access to key findings which often are restricted by a slow academic peer-review process

To give a practical example, I was recently involved in a multi-team collaboration conducting research to develop a satirical measure of 'offline friend addiction' (Satchell, Fido, Harper, Shaw, Davidson, Ellis et al., 2021). Prior to publication in a peer-reviewed journal, the research was made available to the public as a pre-print on the Open Science Framework, and we used a number of methods to share our insights. This consisted of a Tweet-thread by the lead author (Satchell, 2021), with an accompanying blog-post (Harper, 2020) and animation on YouTube (Kaye, 2020) by other members of the research team. Each of these helped us highlight summary points to be made available to the public, largely facilitated by Twitter. Not only were these insights brought into the public realm in a timely way (avoiding the delay related to the peer-review process of academic publishing), they could also be disseminated more widely.

An alternative approach is to make more effective use of public-facing resources such as Wikipedia to widen the availability of scientific evidence to the public. Recently, researchers have begun to make effective use of platforms such as Wikipedia to increase their visibility, especially those who might be considered under-represented in their discipline. An example is Dr Jess Wade who, for the last few years, has written daily updates on Wikipedia and added Wiki entries of women scientists to showcase their contributions (see Howgego, 2020). These platforms, therefore, could be used to showcase the subject area of cyberpsychology to a wider audience. However, there is a note of caution here, given the potential for agenda-driven or biased editing that violates Wikipedia's 'neutral point of view' policy (Martin, 2017).

Finally, the above approaches are not intended to rival the traditional peer-review process, but to complement it.

Collaborations with the media

As mentioned earlier, the media has a substantial role to play in disseminating cyberpsychology research to the general public, as well as practitioners and policy-makers. Unfortunately, journalists are often considered irresponsible or biased in their reporting, only plugging the most 'news-worthy' stories. However, this does a great disservice to the many responsible professionals who provide good-quality coverage of a wide range of issues.

Given the expertise that journalists have in engaging creatively with the public in a variety of ways, they are best placed to help us in the science dissemination process. Researchers may find this is best achieved by having an open online presence (e.g. public Twitter profile, personal website, LinkedIn, Wikipedia page) and engaging in meaningful online networking activities.

Collaborations with journalists and science writers can be especially helpful in the context of research exercises such as the 'Research Excellence Framework' (REF; HEFCE, 2021), a national exercise to assess the quality of research in UK institutions. One element of this relates to research impact, and how research insights may impact on policy, public debate, practitioners, and so on. As cyberpsychology has so much to offer a wide range of beneficiaries, it makes sense to collaborate with others to help disseminate our findings. I conducted my own impact case study to illustrate this in practical terms.

Most of my own research has public beneficiaries as the key stakeholders and so media collaborations have been immensely useful in supporting me to do impactful work. Recent examples have included giving expert commentary for a BBC Trending (2020) piece about online trolling. Here, my insights from my work on social identity and how this may apply online were helpful in communicating how this may operate in cases of online trolling. Other collaborations have been set up in a more strategic way to enable me to provide evidence of impact. These have been supported by my good working relationships with colleagues in the university's press team. For example, I had recently published some research on the psychological benefits of using WhatsApp (Kaye & Quinn, 2020), and sent the details of this to the press office who subsequently put out a press release. This was then picked up by a number of national news organisations including *The Independent* (2020) and *Stylist Magazine* (2020), which have a substantial readership. These two examples, as well as many other media engagements, were presented as evidence of the reach of my research impact within my university's REF (2021) submission.

A great example which draws together the processes of 'academic rigour' and 'journalistic flair' is *The Conversation*. This website allows researchers to author news pieces relating to their expertise in collaboration with *The Conversation*'s journalists, who support the researchers to make the writing accessible and engaging. Recent examples where cyberpsychology insights have gained significant exposure via *The Conversation* include those on cyberbullying (Macaulay, 2020), 'sadfishing' (Hand, 2019), and misinformation via social media (Vijaykumar, 2019).

For a field like cyberpsychology which has a prominent societal role, all these methods of external engagement can serve a useful purpose in helping academic evidence reach a wider range of public beneficiaries, practitioners, and policy-makers.

Policy

In addition to media and public debate, cyberpsychology also has a critical role in informing government policy and regulation. A recent example of this is the UK Online Harms White Paper (HM Government, 2019), which sought to address how to better regulate technology companies. This has been supplemented by the Online Safety Bill (2020), which seeks to legislate against social media firms that do not comply with appropriate standards of duty of care to their users.

As noted in Chapter 8, a lot of cyberpsychology research is focused on online harms (especially in relation to social media), which is relevant here to highlight concerns about why these policies are important. Indeed, the evidence-base for these has recently informed a UK Government inquiry surrounding the mental health impacts of living online (UK Parliament, 2021). Additionally, cyberpsychology insights relating to online social interactions, 'digital divides', digital monitoring, and the health and educational impacts of technology are part of the policy recommendations.

As well as the aforementioned policy surrounding regulating online harms and optimising online living, other recent policy priorities have included regulating immersive and addictive technologies. A recent UK Government inquiry (HM Government, 2020) drew on a range of cyberpsychology evidence in the areas of technological addiction, online gambling, gaming disorder, and the impacts of 'loot boxes' in particular, to inform key recommendations to policy-makers about how such technologies should be best regulated.

There are of course many other ways in which cyberpsychological evidence can and will be used to inform policy recommendations and decisions, and so the need for researchers to conduct timely, good quality, and transparent research is of critical importance.

Practice

As well as the public and policy-makers, practitioners and industry are also key beneficiaries of cyberpsychology research. Some of the most relevant sectors include defence and security, mental health charities and non-profit organisations, e-commerce, digital marketing, and public health. In relation to well-being charities and networks, the eNurture Network is a good example of a catalyst for this, which brings together professionals, researchers, and partners to support evidence-informed practice for promoting young people's mental health in a digital world. Similarly, the TEAM ITN (Technology Enabled Mental Health) network is a consortium of researchers, partners, and not-for-profit organisations to design, develop, and evaluate new technology-enabled mental health services. Indeed, there is a role for cyberpsychologists in informing technological solutions not only for mental health, but a range of human experiences.

In respect of defence and security, cyberpsychology and cybersecurity can help support the work of government departments, such as the Ministry of Defence and the Home Office. In addition, networks such as CybSafe, which supports collaborations between researchers, data analysts, and software engineers, and SPRITE+, which draws together researchers, practitioners, and policy-makers, are excellent networks for best practice in issues such as online security, privacy, identity, and trust. Cybersecurity also has a key role for many businesses, especially large organisations which may practise remote or distributed working.

Finally, cyberpsychology insights are entirely relevant for online marketing and e-commerce, in which understanding usability and the user experience are paramount to effective and accessible marketing and advertising strategies. This consists of user research to explore issues such as user trust, as well as digital analytics to ascertain effective internet searching parameters and users' website behaviour.

Doing impactful research

The above impacts of cyberpsychology relating to the public, policy, and practice can enable researchers in this area to conduct impactful research. In the UK, Higher Education Institutions are assessed on the quality of their research through exercises such as the Research Excellence Framework (HEFCE, 2021). Part of how quality is judged is based on how academic research can be impactful beyond academia, such as informing public debate, developing policy, improving practice, and so on. There is therefore a significant role which cyberpsychology research can fill. In Table 11.1, I use my own impact case study as an example of how cyberpsychology research has been used in previous REF exercises. This provides examples of impact-related activities and associated evidence to help support the *reach* (quantity: how many people, numbers) and *significance* (quality: what has changed) of research impact.

Conclusion

This chapter has outlined three of the prominent impact areas of cyberpsychology research: public debate, policy, and practice. The potential for cyberpsychology to be impactful will be facilitated by researchers being open and transparent in the research process, making their research findings as accessible as possible, and collaborating with other relevant stakeholders (e.g. the media). Of course, all relevant codes of ethics and standards must be strictly adhered to, including the principles of respect, competence, responsibility, and

Table 11.1 Case study with examples of impact activities and evidence

Beneficiary	Purpose	Underpinning research	Impact activity	Type of impact	Examples of evidence
Public	Widening public understanding and debate	Wall, Kaye, & Malone (2016)	Media engagement (various)	Reach	The Conversation views SciShow (YouTube show) views TEDxTalk attendance and YouTube views
Public	Widening public understanding and debate	Wall et al. (2016); Wall, Kaye, & Malone (2016)	Media engagement (various)	Significance	Quotes from comments from TEDx Talk on YouTube Quotes and public comments in media presenter's blog post about emoji
Public	Widening public understanding and debate	Wall et al. (2016); Kaye et al. (2016); Darbyshire, Kirk, Wall, & Kaye (2016); Kaye, Wall, & Hird (2020)	Public engagement events (Psychology in the Pub sessions on 'What your emoji says about you')	Significance	Delegate quiz results about level of understanding
Public	Widening public understanding and debate	Kaye, Carlisle, & Griffiths (2019); Kaye, Kowert, & Quinn (2017)	Media engagement (with BBC Trending on expert commentary on online trolling)	Reach	Twitter metrics and threads News page views
Public	Informing public behaviour change	Wall, Campbell, Kaye, Levy, & Bhullar (2019)	PR campaign (with Change Incorporated to develop a non-smoking emoji to encourage smoking cessation)	Reach	Social media video content metrics

Table 11.1 (Continued)

Beneficiary	Purpose	Underpinning research	Impact activity	Type of impact	Examples of evidence
Public	Informing public behaviour change	Wall et al. (2019)	Consultancy (with *Which?* Magazine to give expert comment on online scam victim testimonials)	Significance Reach	Testimonial from *Which?* Video content metrics
Businesses	Informing business behaviour change	Wall et al. (2019)	Consultancy (with Trend Micro on developing a persona-based taxonomy for mitigating cybersecurity risks during remote working)	Significance Significance Reach	Testimonial from Trend Micro White Paper/Report with recommendations Trade press readership metrics
Businesses	Informing business behaviour change	Kaye & Quinn (2020)	Consultancy (with InsideOut on the development and evaluation of a mental health disclosure app)	Significance Significance Reach	Citation in evidence review Testimonial from CEO of InsideOut Pilot update with businesses
Policy-makers	Contribution to policy	Kaye & Quinn (2020)	Invited to give Parliamentary oral evidence (on the mental health impacts of living online)	Significance Significance Significance	Testimonial from BPS Policy team Written transcript of oral evidence session Associated social media content of evidence

integrity (e.g. BPS Code of Ethics and Conduct, 2018). First and foremost, cyberpsychologists are psychologists, but with specialist subject knowledge and skill-sets pertaining to cyberpsychology issues. As yet, no regulatory body recognises 'cyberpsychologist' as a protected title in the same way that 'clinical psychologist' is registered with the Health and Care Professions Council (HCPC), for example. Thus, not only do we have a role in promoting the field of cyberpsychology, we must also present ourselves in the best light, especially within the public sphere.

Box 11.1: Thinking activity

- What practical advice would you recommend to researchers in cyberpsychology to make their insights more visible and/or accessible to the public?
- List those organisations and/or sectors that you feel would benefit from cyberpsychology insights.

Box 11.2: Take-home message

Cyberpsychology has a prominent role to play in twenty-first-century society, and researchers in this area must ensure their work is visible and accessible to the public, practitioners, and policy-makers alike. Cyberpsychology will only increase in relevance, and so being forward-thinking is critical to ensuring its standing and practical value.

References

BBC Trending (2020). *What happened when a troll met his target?* Retrieved 8 January 2021 from: https://www.bbc.co.uk/sounds/play/w3csyvpb

British Psychological Society (BPS) (2018). *Code of ethics and conduct.* Leicester: BPS. https://www.bps.org.uk/sites/bps.org.uk/files/Policy%20-%20Files/BPS%20Code%20 of%20Ethics%20and%20Conduct%20%28Updated%20July%202018%29.pdf

Darbyshire, D.E., Kirk, C., Wall, H.J., & Kaye, L.K. (2016). Don't judge a (Face)book by its cover: Exploring judgement accuracy of others' personality on Facebook. *Computers in Human Behavior, 58,* 380–387. https://doi.org/10.1016/j.chb.2016.01.021

Hand, C. (2019). *Sadfishing: Frequently sharing deeply emotional posts online may be a sign of a deeper psychological issue.* Retrieved 7 January 2021 from: https://theconversation.com/sadfishing-frequently-sharing-deeply-emotional-posts-online-may-be-a-sign-of-a-deeper-psychological-issue-126292

Harper, C. (2020). *O-FAQ … We're all addicted to our friends?! Our new study confirms issues with 'addiction' classification* [Blog post]. Retrieved from: https://medium.com/open-psychological-science/o-faq-were-all-addicted-to-our-friends-a6b5f1df5810

HEFCE (2021). *REF 2021: Research Excellence Framework*. Retrieved 7 July 2021 from: https://www.ref.ac.uk

HM Government (2019). *Online Harms White Paper*. Retrieved 15 June 15 2019 from: https://assets.publishing.service.gov.uk/government/uploads/system/uploads/attachment_data/file/793360/Online_Harms_White_Paper.pdf

HM Government (2020) *Government response to the Digital, Culture, Media and Sport Select Committee Report on Immersive and Addictive Technologies*, CP 241. London: The Stationery Office. Retrieved 7 January 2021 from: https://assets.publishing.service.gov.uk/government/uploads/system/uploads/attachment_data/file/890734/CCS207_CCS0520664408-001_Gov_Resp_DCMS_Committee_Report_CP_241_Web_Accessible__1___1_.pdf

Howgego, J. (2020). Jess Wade's one-woman mission to diversify Wikipedia's science stories. *New Scientist*, 3268. https://www.newscientist.com/article/mg24532680-800-jess-wades-one-woman-mission-to-diversify-wikipedias-science-stories/

Kaye, L.K. (2020). Offline friend addiction [Video]. *YouTube*, 19 March. https://www.youtube.com/watch?v=KJ8CWk6GPFg

Kaye, L.K., Carlisle, C.R., & Griffiths, L.R.W. (2019). A contextual account of the psychosocial impacts of social identity in a sample of digital gamers. *Psychology of Popular Media Culture, 8* (3), 259–268. https://doi.org/10.1037/ppm0000173

Kaye, L.K., Kowert, R., & Quinn, S. (2017). The role of social identity and online social capital on psychosocial outcomes in MMO players. *Computers in Human Behavior, 74*, 215–223. https://doi.org/10.1016/j.chb.2017.04.030

Kaye, L.K., & Quinn, S. (2020). Psychosocial outcomes associated with engagement with online chat systems. *International Journal of Human-Computer Interaction, 36* (2), 190–198. https://doi.org/10.1080/10447318.2019.1620524

Kaye, L.K., Wall, H.J., & Hird, A.T. (2020). Less is more when rating Extraversion: Behavioural cues and interpersonal perceptions on the platform of Facebook. *Psychology of Popular Media, 9* (4), 465–474. https://doi.org/10.1037/ppm0000263

Kaye, L.K., Wall, H.J., & Malone, S.A. (2016). 'Turn that frown upside-down': A contextual account of emoticon usage on different virtual platforms. *Computers in Human Behavior, 60*, 463–467. https://doi.org/10.1016/j.chb.2016.02.088

Macaulay, P. (2020). *We don't know the true extent of cyberbullying – and children need help in dealing with it*. Retrieved 7 January 2021 from: https://theconversation.com/we-dont-know-the-true-extent-of-cyberbullying-and-children-need-help-in-dealing-with-it-131614

Martin, B. (2017). Persistent bias on Wikipedia: Methods and responses. *Social Science Computer Review, 36* (3), 379–388. https://doi.org/10.1177/0894439317715434

Satchell, L. [@lpsatchell] (2020). New paper! Are you missing spending time with your friends? Perhaps during this time of self-isolation you need to be ... [Tweet]. *Twitter*, 18 March. https://twitter.com/lpsatchell/status/1240202782403186688

Satchell, L., Fido, D., Harper, C., Shaw, H., Davidson, B.I., Ellis, D.A. et al. (2021). Development of an Offline-Friend Addiction Questionnaire (O-FAQ): Are most people really social addicts? *Behavior Research Methods, 53*, 1097–1106. https://doi.org/10.3758/s13428-020-01462-9

Stylist Magazine (2020). *Why WhatsApp might actually be good for your mental health*. Retrieved 8 January 2021 from: https://www.stylist.co.uk/life/whatsapp-mental-health-benefits-social-media-contact-friends-family-wellbeing/277833

The Independent (2020). *WhatsApp is good for your health, new research claims*. Retrieved 8 January 2021 from: https://www.independent.co.uk/life-style/gadgets-and-tech/news/whatsapp-mental-health-screen-time-social-media-wellbeing-a8982681.html

UK Parliament (2021). *Beyond digital: Planning for a hybrid world.* Retrieved 24 April 2021 from: https://publications.parliament.uk/pa/ld5801/ldselect/ldcvd19/263/26302.htm

Vijaykumar, S. (2019). *Pseudoscience is taking over social media – and putting us all at risk.* Retrieved 7 January 2021 from: https://theconversation.com/amp/pseudoscience-is-taking-over-social-media-and-putting-us-all-at-risk-121062?__twitter_impression=true

Wall, H.J., Campbell, C., Kaye, L.K., Levy, A.R., & Bhullar, N. (2019). Personality profiles and persuasion: An exploratory study investigating the role of the Big-5, Type D personality and the Dark Triad on susceptibility to persuasion. *Personality and Individual Differences, 139,* 69–75. https://doi.org/10.1016/j.paid.2018.11.003

Wall, H.J., Kaye, L.K., & Malone, S.A. (2016). An exploration of psychological factors on emoticon usage and implications for judgement accuracy. *Computers in Human Behavior, 62,* 70–78. https://doi.org/10.1016/j.chb.2016.03.040

12 Conclusion and the future of cyberpsychology

This book has presented key societal and academic debates in the area of cyberpsychology, including so-called 'screen-time' effects, digital gaming effects, online vs. offline behaviour, and so on. There is a common thread to all of these – namely, that these debates are plagued by dichotomies. As a result, there are unhelpful divides in thinking and sentiment, creating both conceptual and practical problems in advancing our understanding of these issues. Whilst some debate is useful for stimulating scientific enquiry, the presence of polarisation, as is the case in many of the debates covered in this book, really is a step too far. Much of this stems from our adoption of technology-centred approaches, such as measuring volume of technology use (time, frequency), to the detriment of the rich interactions and behaviours that are clearly evident as well as user-centred perspectives, such as asking 'why'.

Problems clearly exist at a basic conceptual level, reflected in the terminology used and a lack of coherence in the conceptual basis of what we mean by 'technology use'. It is no surprise that these issues translate into problems in the way 'technology use' and online behaviour are measured and how these are theorised in respect of user experiences and impacts. It is entirely likely that our current scientific understanding of technology use and psychology is flawed, or, at the very least, under-explored in respect of us having a clear consensus on how certain technological behaviours are best measured. We need to remember that 'technology use' can refer to a lot of things and is a complex process (adoption, continued use, specific usage behaviours). Therefore, finding conceptual agreement on how this fits together is paramount if the field is to progress.

From a conceptual point of view, a move away from using prefixes (e.g. online, cyber, e, Internet, digital, etc.) will help to avoid the unhelpful categorisation of behaviours simply based on whether they take place via a screen or not. Prefixes such as these immediately create a dichotomy with 'analogue', not a particularly helpful approach when we want to understand how our everyday experiences can be garnered through technology and aspects of the internet. Advances in these debates can certainly be enabled by looking beyond surface behaviours of using screens. In digital society, it is becoming more challenging to categorise ourselves and our behaviours based on whether they are 'online' or 'offline', as the boundary between the two is no longer so distinct. It is better to avoid such categorisations and instead explore behaviour itself and how this manifests (perhaps differently) under different conditions and in different contexts. This is especially relevant when we consider the extent to which our 'online data' can be revealing of behaviours which are not just taking place online.

Cyberpsychology researchers are psychologists first and foremost, and so we have to make sure our research enquiries are psychologically interesting and explanatory. Focusing exclusively on time spent using technology as a metric is not an interesting line of enquiry. Screen-time as an example of this does not offer a psychological explanation behind our technology use based on the wide range of experiences afforded to us. From a psychological perspective, understanding usage – why we use technology, what purpose it fulfils, and so on – is much more interesting. Objective data can allow us accurate insights into screen-time, perhaps unlike subjective reports, but this is only one aspect of a much broader question relating to screen use. We will also be much better equipped to answer questions about the range of experiences and effects of technology use.

Of course, one of the ongoing challenges of studying technology and the internet is its dynamic nature. Not only does technology change rapidly, the internet is a largely dynamic entity, where an individual's use is far from static and stable. Unlike more traditional types of media such as newspapers and TV, Web 2.0 is interactional and multifunctional. Human behaviour in respect of the internet cannot therefore be considered an individually driven experience or set of behaviours. It is constantly shaped by other individuals, groups, social technology solutions, politics, economics, and legal infrastructures. Whilst much of the current scientific and public understanding of technology use tends to theorise it at an individual level, we will only advance our understanding of its nature and effects by considering it at a societal level. I recognise that this book has drawn on a number of recommended frameworks. Figure 12.1 is intended to bring these together to represent the range of

Figure 12.1. Consolidated framework for visualising the range of factors and processes to understand effects of technology and internet use

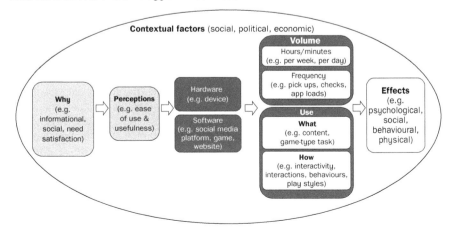

factors and processes relevant for understanding technology and internet use from the perspective of their effects. The dark grey boxes represent technology-centred concerns, whilst the light grey boxes represent user-centred issues. As you can see, these tend not to be exclusive of one another and they can each contribute something useful in understanding psychological experiences and effects of technology use.

In my introductory chapter, I outlined that cyberpsychology typically covers three main areas: (1) our motivations for using technology and aspects of the internet; (2) how we interact with technology and others via the internet; and (3) the effects and impacts associated with using technology and the internet. I am hopeful that the framework in Figure 12.1 can help us appreciate how these all relate to one another. At the far left are the main reasons or motivations for use. These include need satisfaction, occupational demands, or simply a way of passing time. Next, there are various perceptions or attitudes that relate to which devices and/or platforms to use to fulfil certain needs, particularly at the technology acceptance/adoption stage. Use can also be explored based on things like types of interactions. As noted throughout, this is a complex phenomenon and is often studied with respect to time spent accessing technology or activities on the internet. However, time/frequency of use is only one part of the equation and is not the most psychologically interesting part. Instead, we are better placed to understand the range of uses by exploring the 'what' and 'how' of our interactions. Some of this may be made apparent through time-based metrics using screen-time apps or objective data logs, but a range of additional measures are required to more fully access the range of available behaviours. Only from our exploration of these complex uses and behaviours will we better understand the full range of effects. Alongside this, to make the leap between technology uses and effects, especially behavioural effects, there needs to be a more concerted effort to integrate robust behaviour change frameworks to ensure the expected effects are underpinned theoretically. These may include the COM-B system (Michie, van Stralen, & West, 2011), which can account for a range of factors and processes expected to relate to behavioural effects.

Moving from the conceptual to the practical, researchers need to use more intricate and/or objective approaches when measuring different types of online behaviours or technology use. For example, our understanding of how social media use relates to well-being cannot be established without measuring specific types of interactions and behaviours (which may in some cases be garnered objectively) and how these correspond psychologically and socially. Using a basic measure of 'how often do you use Facebook?', for example, is no way sufficient to advance our knowledge of this. This is the case for most types of technology, including social media and digital games, in that we need to know more about the 'what', 'how', and 'why' to improve our understanding of the range of experiences and effects. I refer to this here as the 'WHW' framework. Table 12.1 provides some examples to illustrate this approach, which I hope will provide some practical suggestions for future research on these issues.

Table 12.1 Indicative examples of how pertinent research questions can be approached using the WHW framework

	Technology-centred			User-centred
	Focus	**What**	**How**	**Why**
Issue 1: Motivations for using technology and the Internet				
How much do we use our smartphones?	Smartphones Categories of app use App use	Distinguish the apps or categories of apps being used	What is our overall daily/weekly screen-time? What is our overall daily/weekly screen-time on different categories of apps? (e.g. productivity, social, games, etc.) What is our overall daily/weekly screen-time on specific apps?	Are there times and places we are more likely to use our smartphones or specific types of apps than others? (weekday vs. weekend, familiar place vs. new place, alone vs. with others)?
Issue 2: How we interact with technology and others via the Internet				
Is 'active use' (vs. 'passive use') a typology of user (trait) or context-specific behaviour?	Applied to any specific social media platform	Type of content engaged with	Distinguishing behaviours which relate to various levels of interactive use, and establish whether these remain stable for people across platforms	Why may we be more likely to engage in different levels of interaction on social media? Does this vary by type of content? Does this vary by audience/recipient of action?

Table 12.1   *(Continued)*

Issue 3: Effects and impacts associated with using technology and the internet

To what extent do smartphones cause a distraction during work/study?	Smartphones	Notifications	Distinguish how smartphone use varies when push notifications are activated vs. deactivated
		App downtime settings	Establish how this use corresponds to different study/work contexts (individual vs group work, home vs. work-related contexts, self-study vs. timetabled/classroom settings)
		Specific types of apps (e.g. social media)	Establish how this use corresponds to different study/work parameters (urgent vs. non-urgent work, important vs. non-important work, level of interest in work)
			Are smartphones being used as a general distraction (to pass the time, procrastinate) or smartphone-initiated (alerts/notifications)?
How do our smartphones impact our memory capacities?	Internet searching	Do people use information-searching on their smartphones for a semantic memory aid?	How much do people use information-searching to help semantic memory/recall?
	Social media memories	Do people use social media platforms that include social media memory features (e.g. Facebook, Instagram) for an episodic memory aid?	How much are people exposed to social media memories?
	Instant notes	Do people use instant notes on their smartphone for a prospective memory aid?	How much do people use instant notes on their smartphone to aid their prospective memory?
			Why are we likely to do an internet search for a semantic memory aid rather than assume we may remember something subsequently?
			Do we use prospective memory aids on smartphones (e.g. notes) because we believe we will forget when needed or because the act of noting it is helpful for forming a memory?

| Is using social media bad for self-esteem and/or body image? | Image-based social media (TikTok, Instagram) | Distinguishing between types of content; developing a codebook for content (landscapes, faces, bodies, animals, etc.)

Proportionality and/or number of accounts someone follows which may be body- or beauty-focused | Establish how much time proportionally on using image-based platforms is spent being exposed to body- or beauty-related content | Why do we follow certain accounts?

To what extent do different types of social comparisons (upwards vs. downward) from image-based social media use impact on continued use and/or the following of certain accounts? |
| How do different types of engagement on social media impact on human relationships? | Applied to any specific social media platform | Type of content engaged with

Personal vs. professional use

Personal vs. organisational use (e.g. digital marketers)

Platform variations

Network maps of within- and between-network ties (to denote social ties and/or social capital)

Distinguish between social media time (frequency/time) and social media use (behaviours, interactions) | Distinguishing behaviours which relate to different levels of interactivity | Why may we be more likely to engage in different levels of interaction on social media?

Does this vary by type of content?

Does this vary by audience/recipient of action?

Why do we use social media? |

Table 12.1   (Continued)

What is the role of social media in disinformation?	Applied to any specific social media platform	What type of content/topics are most prone to be presented as disinformation? How is this presented on social media (news article, fake photo/video, etc.)? What are the characteristics to help distinguish disinformation content?	To what extent are social media engagement metrics on disinformation content (e.g. likes, etc.) related to how we behaviourally react to content (e.g. like, angry reactions, sharing, reposting)? How does 'who' has previously shared impact on our likelihood to interact with disinformation content (someone respectable, authority, etc.)?	Why are some people more susceptible to disinformation than others?
How does digital gaming relate to well-being?	Applied to any specific type of digital game/gaming	Distinguish type/genre of game Structural components of games and their relevance for well-being	Play patterns (hardcore, casual) Level of 'socialness' of games and gaming behaviours	Why do players engage with these games (e.g. professionally, for leisure, for health)?

As you can see from Table 12.1, there are a range of considerations in respect of WHW which can be addressed through empirical research to acknowledge some of the intricacies involved. The examples of smartphones, social media, and digital gaming are highlighted, but the same principles could apply across a broader range of platforms. Ideally, all of the components of the WHW framework should be incorporated into research programmes on these issues, although it may not be the case that single studies themselves can achieve this. However, I see the WHW framework as a conceptual tool for researchers when planning research programmes to map these key components into an integrated framework.

Advancing the conceptual and methodological bases for cyberpsychology work is not just important academically. Indeed, the public-facing nature of the issues covered in this field requires sound science. This research not only has a role in informing public debate on these issues, but also in influencing practice and policy. We should not settle for 'evidence-informed' policy or practice, but rather 'scientifically-sound informed' practices. Unfortunately, currently these can often look quite different.

Although cyberpsychology is well placed to help us answer a lot of questions about human behaviour, there is a long way to go. Cyberpsychology has a prominent place in twenty-first-century society, and researchers in this area have to ensure their insights are visible and accessible to the public, practitioners, and policy-makers alike. This is especially relevant when we consider the extent to which our 'online data' is out in the world, being collected and used for a multitude of purposes. Cyberpsychology is likely to only increase in relevance, and so being forward-thinking on these mechanisms will be critical to ensuring it can be useful and of practical value.

Reference

Michie, S., van Stralen, M.M., & West, R. (2011). The behaviour change wheel: A new method for characterising and designing behaviour change interventions. *Implementation Science, 6*, 42. https://doi.org/10.1186/1748-5908-6-42

Index